Content Overview

The Quick College Guide is composed of seven parts that offer chapters on various aspects of reading, writing, studying, research, documentation, life skills, and language skills.

Part I. Reading and Study Skills. This section includes chapters on previewing a textbook and a chapter, reading and studying a textbook, listening to lectures and taking notes, participating in class, collaborative learning, and test taking.

Part II. Basic Writing Skills. Writing is the theme of this section, and a number of topics, traditional and otherwise, are covered. It begins with writing college essays and papers and goes on to cover writing effective paragraphs, journal writing, responsive writing (analysis), writing laboratory or field reports, writing case study analyses, and writing abstracts and executive summaries.

Part III. Basic Document Design and Format. This section briefly outlines the design and standard formats for college papers, business letters, memorandum, and e-mail—the most common document formats.

Part IV. Research and Writing Research Papers. The four chapters in this section explain basic research methods, Internet research, evaluating Internet sources, and writing research papers.

Part V. Documentation. This section clarifies the necessity and requirements of documentation and cautions against plagiarism. The two most commonly used documentation methods taught in college, MLA and APA, are described.

Part VI. Life Skills. The chapters in this section discuss various valuable life skills and situations, such as goal setting, time management, resources management, diversity, and disabilities.

Part VII. Language Skills. This final section covers the basics of the parts of speech, sentence structure, and punctuation.

Appendix. The appendix covers the structure of a formal argument for research papers.

Chapter Organization and Features

The chapters in *The Quick College Guide* follow a basic, flexible pattern.

- Chapter title
- List of steps or suggested methods
- Instruction and discussion, matched to steps
- Samples or examples, where appropriate
- Exercises or Discussion Questions, where appropriate

The chapters contain various features that help illustrate what is being discussed, including the numbering and matching of steps, marked reading text, examples, writing samples, sample formats, exercises and discussion questions. These features enhance the text material for both instructor and students.

The Ancillary Package

For Additional Reading and Reference

The Dictionary Deal. Two dictionaries can be shrinkwrapped with any Longman Basic Skills title at a nominal fee: *The New American Webster Handy College Dictionary* (paperback) and *Merriam Webster's Collegiate Dictionary* (hardback).

Penguin Quality Paperback Titles. A series of Penguin paperbacks is available at a significant discount when shrinkwrapped with any Longman title. For a complete list of titles or more information, please contact your Longman sales consultant.

The Pocket Reader and *The Brief Pocket Reader,* **First Edition.** These inexpensive volumes contain 80 brief readings and 50 readings, respectively. *The Pocket Reader*: ISBN 0-321-07668-0; *The Brief Pocket Reader*: ISBN 0-321-07669-9.

100 Things to Write About. This pamphlet contains 100 individual assignments for writing on a variety of topics and in a wide range of formats, from expressive to analytical. ISBN 0-673-98239-4.

The Longman Textbook Reader. This supplement offers five complete chapters from Addison Wesley/Longman textbooks: computer science, biology, psychology, communications, and business. Each chapter includes additional comprehension quizzes, critical thinking questions, and group activities. Available in two formats: with answers and without answers.

Newsweek **Alliance.** Instructors may choose to shrinkwrap a 12-week subscription to *Newsweek* with any Longman text. The price of the subscription is 59 cents per issue (a total of $7.08 for the subscription). Available with the subscription is a free "Interactive Guide to *Newsweek,*" a workbook for students who are using the text.

Electronic and Online Offerings

The Longman Study Skills Web site. This Web site is the perfect accompaniment to any freshman orientation, study skills, or reading course. If offers a wealth of resources, exercises, and Web links to help students make the most of their college courses and college experience. Visit the Web site at **http://www.ablongman. com/studyskills.**

The Longman Writer's Warehouse. The innovative and exciting online supplement is the perfect accompaniment to any developmental writing course. The Writer's Warehouse covers every part of the writing process. Also included are journaling capabilities, multimedia activities, diagnostic tests, an interactive handbook, and a complete instructor's manual. For a free guided tour of the site, visit **http://longmanwriterswarehouse.com.**

The Writers ToolKit Plus. This CD-ROM offers a wealth of tutorial, exercise, and reference material for writers.

GrammarCoach Software. This interactive tutorial helps students practice the basics of grammar and punctuation through 600 self-grading exercises in such problems areas as fragments, run-ons, and agreement.

Longman Reading Road Trip Multimedia Software, CD Version and Web Version. This innovative multimedia reading software is available either on CD-ROM format or on the Web. The package takes students on a tour of 15 cities and landmarks throughout the United States. Each of the 15 modules corresponds to a reading or study skill (for example, finding the main idea, understanding patterns of organization, and thinking critically). All modules contain a tour of the location, instruction and tutorial, exercises, interactive feedback, and mastery tests.

Longman Vocabulary Web site. For a wealth of vocabulary-related resources, visit our free vocabulary Web site at **http:// www.ablongman.com/vocabulary.**

The Longman Electronic Newsletter. Twice per month during the spring and fall, instructors who have subscribed receive a free copy of the Longman Developmental English Newsletter in their e-mailbox. To subscribe, send an e-mail to **Basic Skills@ablongman.com.**

For Instructors

Electronic Test Bank for Writing. This electronic test bank features more than 5,000 questions in all areas of writing, from grammar to paragraphing, through essay writing, research, and documentation. With this easy-to-use CD-ROM, instructors simply choose questions from the electronic test bank, then print out the completed test for distribution.

Electronic Test Bank for Reading. This electronic test bank offers more than 3,000 questions in all areas of reading, including vocabulary, main idea, supporting details, patterns of organization, language, critical thinking, analytical reasoning, inference, point of view, visual aids, and textbook reading. With this easy-to-use CD-ROM, instructors simply choose questions from the electronic test bank, then print out the completed test for distribution.

Competency Profile Test Bank, Second Edition. This series of 60 objective tests covers ten general areas of English competency, including fragments; comma splices and run-ons; pronouns; commas; and capitalization. Each test is available in remedial, standard, and advanced versions.

Diagnostic and Editing Tests and Exercises, Fifth Edition. This collection of diagnostic tests helps instructors assess students competence in Standard Written English for the purpose of placement or to gauge progress. Available as reproducible sheets or in computerized versions.

ESL Worksheets, Third Edition. These reproducible worksheets provide ESL students with extra practice in areas they find the most troublesome. A diagnostic test and post-test are provided, along with answer keys and suggested topics for writing.

Longman Editing Exercises. A total of 54 pages of paragraph editing exercises give students extra practice using grammar skills in the context of longer passages. Free when packaged with any Longman title.

80 Practices. A collection of reproducible, ten-item exercises that provide additional practices for specific grammatical usage problems, such as comma splices, capitalization, and pronouns. Includes an answer key.

CLAST Test Package, Fourth Edition. These two 40-item objective tests evaluate students' readiness for the CLAST exams. Strategies for teaching CLAST preparedness are included.

TASP Test Package, Third Edition. These 12 practice pre-tests and post-tests assess the same reading and writing skills covered in the TASP examination. Free with any Longman English Title.

Teaching Online: Internet Research, Conversation, and Composition, Second Edition. Ideal for instructors who have never surfed the Net, this easy-to-follow guide offers basic definitions, numerous examples, and step-by-step information about finding and using Internet sources.

Teaching Writing to the Non-Native Speaker. This booklet examines the issues that arise when non-native speakers enter the developmental classroom. Free to instructors, it includes profiles of international and permanent ESL students, factors influencing second-language acquisition, and tips on managing a multicultural classroom.

Using Portfolios. This supplement offers teachers a brief introduction to teaching with portfolios in composition courses. This essential guide addresses the pedagogical and evaluative use of portfolios, and offers practical suggestions for implementing a portfolio evaluation system in a writing class.

For Students

Researching Online, Fifth Edition. A perfect companion for a new age, this indispensable new supplement helps students navigate the Internet. Adapted from *Teaching Online,* the instructor's Internet guide, *Researching Online* speaks directly to students, giving them detailed, step-by-step instructions for performing electronic searches.

Learning Together: An Introduction to Collaborative Theory. This brief guide to the fundamentals of collaborative learning teaches students how to work effectively in groups, how to revise with peer response, and how to co-author a paper or report.

A Guide for Peer Response, Second Edition. This guide offers students forms for peer critiques, including general guidelines and specific forms for different stages in the writing process.

Thinking Through the Test, by D. J. Henry. This special workbook, prepared specially for students in Florida, offers ample skill and practice exercises to help student prep for the Florida State Exit Exam. Also available: two laminated grids (one for reading, one for writing) that can serve as handy references for students preparing for the Florida State Exit Exam.

The Longman Reader's Journal, by Kathleen T. McWhorter. This reader's journal offers students a space to record their questions about, reactions to, and summaries of materials they've read. Also included is personal vocabulary log, as well as ample space for free writing.

The Longman Writer's Journal. This journal for writers offers students a place to think, write, and react.

The Longman Researcher's Journal. This journal for writers and researchers helps students plan, schedule, write, and revise their research project. An all-in-one resource for first-time researchers, the journal guides students gently through the research process.

NEW! *The Longman Reader's Portfolio.* This unique supplement provides students with a space to plan, think about, and present their work. The portfolio includes a diagnostic area (including a learning style questionnaire), a working area (including calendars, vocabulary logs, reading response sheets, book club tips, and other valuable materials), and a display area (including a progress chart, a final table of contents, and a final assessment).

NEW! *The Longman Writer's Portfolio.* This unique supplement provides students with a space to plan, think about, and present their work. The portfolio includes an assessing/organizing area (including a grammar diagnostic test, a spelling quiz, and project planning worksheets), a before and during writing area (including peer review sheets, editing checklists, writing self-evaluations, and a personal editing profile), and an after-writing area (including a progress chart, a final table of contents, and a final assessment).

Acknowledgments

We wish to acknowledge the contribution of our colleagues who provided valuable advice, assistance, and suggestions:

Bob Boyd, Fresno City College; Donna Chandler, Fresno City College; Nancy Holland, Fresno City College; Linda Jackson, Fresno City College; Jerry Kirkhart, Fresno City College; Craig Poole, Fresno City College; David Racki, Fresno City College; Jeannie Santos, FUSD; William Syvertsen, Fresno City College; and Roberta Wingo, Cedar Productions; and the Fresno City College Library Staff.

We would also like to thank the following reviewers:

Jonathan Alexander, University of Cincinnati; Ann Deprey, University of Wisconsin, Green Bay; Stephanie Hall, Pitt Community College; Lee Herrick, Fresno City College; Richard C. Ingram, Winthrop University; Jenny Joczik, University of South Carolina; John Lundquist, Golden West College, Lisa Orta, Diablo Valley College; Sylvia Newman Pack, Weber State University; James Scruton, Bethel College; and Rae Strickland, Manchester Community College.

We reserve special thanks for our editor, Steven Rigolosi, Senior Acquisitions Editor, and his staff, whose help and encouragement were invaluable.

Clay D. Rooks
Richard A. Santos

Part I:
READING AND STUDY SKILLS

CHAPTER 1
Previewing a Textbook and a Chapter

1. Previewing a Textbook
   1.1 Front Cover
   1.2 Back Cover
   1.3 Notes to the Student
   1.4 Notes to the Teacher
   1.5 Preface/Introduction
   1.6 Table of Contents
   1.7 Appendixes
   1.8 Index

2. Previewing a Chapter
   2.1 Chapter Objectives
   2.2 Title and Headers
   2.3 Pictures, Charts, and Graphs
   2.4 Boldface, Italics, Margin Notes, and Chapter Glossaries
   2.5 Summaries

1. PREVIEWING A TEXTBOOK

Being a student takes a lot of time and effort. College reading assignments are often quite challenging. Unfortunately, when it comes to reading, many students skip one of the most important steps in reading text-books: previewing. If students jump directly into reading without first trying to understand how the text is organized and what the author's purpose is, many times they will not fully understand the concepts that are being explained. By following the steps for previewing listed below, you can become focused and efficient in your reading.

1.1 Front Cover

Read the front cover of the text for title and author.

1.2 Back Cover

After checking the front cover, flip the book over and read the back cover of the text for an overall summary of what the text is about.

1.3 Notes to the Student

Read "Notes to the Student" if the text has one. This information gives an overview of the text features and how the chapters or units are organized as well as the types of exercises that are found in the text.

1.4 Notes to the Teacher

Read "Notes to the Teacher" if the text has one. This section is similar to "Notes to the Student." However, it may include an explanation of the author's approach and the types of activities teachers could incorporate into their lessons.

1.5 Preface/Introduction

If the text doesn't contain student and teacher notes, there will be a preface or introduction instead. This section contains information about what the book covers, what approach the author uses, how the chapters and exercises are laid out, and any other useful information you might need while reading.

1.6 Table of Contents

Read the "Table of Contents" to see what is covered in each chapter.

1.7 Appendixes

Find the "Appendix" at the back of the text. Although appendixes vary in the information they contain, the following could be found, for example, in a statistics textbook.

Appendixes	
Appendix A	Tables 506
Appendix B	Data Sets 521
Appendix C	Glossary 544
Appendix D	Bibliography 550
Appendix E	Answer Key 556

As mentioned earlier, appendixes vary in their content. Glossaries, bibliographies, and answer keys are three of the most common appendixes.

- **Glossary.** Contains the definitions of terms used in the text (generally the bold and italicized words that appear in each chapter).
- **Bibliography.** Lists authors and/or articles cited in the text. This section can be helpful when doing research because you have at your disposal the names of authors or articles that the text's author used in writing the textbook.
- **Answer Keys.** Some texts supply answer keys to problems found in each chapter. These allow you to check your answers *after* completing the exercises.

Appendixes may also contain additional exercises, charts, maps, suggested activities, and so on, all of which are related to what you are learning from the book.

1.8 Index

Lists names or subjects covered in the book. The index is arranged alphabetically and is very useful when trying to locate a specific person, concept, or idea.

Previewing takes a little time. However, by previewing the entire text, you will save valuable time throughout the semester because you will know how each chapter is organized, where information can be found, and, most important, you will have a more focused purpose.

2. PREVIEWING A CHAPTER

Just as previewing an entire textbook helps you to become a more efficient and focused reader, so does previewing a chapter or unit in a text. Many textbooks now try to be more reader-friendly, that is, they are designed to guide the reader through the material in the text. However, many readers still go directly to the first paragraph and begin reading without any clear idea of what the chapter will be about. By previewing, your focus is sharper because you will know what to look for. Focus on the following steps while previewing.

2.1 Chapter Objectives

The objectives of the chapter are usually listed at the beginning of the chapter. The objectives tell you what points will be covered in the chapter.

2.2 Title and Headers

Look at the titles and headers for each chapter. The title refers to the main idea of the chapter, and the headers refer to the main idea of that section. Before reading the chapter, look over the title and the headers and take a minute to think about what you already know about the topic. This will help you focus and connect new information to what you already know. The following example is taken from a speech communication text.

EXAMPLE: THINKING ABOUT TITLES AND HEADERS

Sample chapter titles:

"Coping with Speech Anxiety"

"Listening Techniques"

"Adapting to the Audience"

Try forming the chapter titles into questions. You might ask yourself questions such as:

What do I know about coping with speech anxiety?

- It is difficult to talk in front of a group of people.
- Ways to cope are to relax, make eye contact, and be prepared.

What do I know about listening techniques?

- I should lean forward and nod my head.

What do I know about adapting to the audience?

- I should know who my audience is before I speak to them.
- I should think of questions the audience might ask and prepare answers before I speak.

2.3 Pictures, Charts, and Graphs

Look at the pictures, charts, or graphs and read the captions. Generally, these graphics reflect one of the main points being discussed and are placed in the text to further explain and clarify these points.

2.4 Boldface or Italicized Type, Margin Notes, and Chapter Glossaries

Many texts use boldface or italicized type to highlight important vocabulary terms and concepts. Some texts include margin notes with the definition or an explanation of terms. Very reader-friendly texts include a short glossary at the end of the chapter containing the definitions and explanations of the terms. Do not ignore these aids because they will help you to understand what you need to study and remember about the chapter.

2.5 Summaries

Many texts include a chapter summary at the end of each chapter, which explains the main points that are discussed in the chapter. Quickly skimming the summary prepares you for finding the main points while reading.

If you preview a chapter before you read, you will know how each chapter is organized and what information it contains. Changing the title and headers into questions can help you focus on finding the important information presented in the chapter. Graphics and summaries refer to the main points. Clearly, previewing a chapter helps you focus your attention on what you need to learn.

Exercise 1.1

Directions: Use a textbook from one of your classes to complete the worksheet below.

1. Write the title of the book. _____

2. What year was the text published? _____

3. What is the edition (e.g., 3rd)? _____

4. Write the names of the authors. _____

5. Read the back cover of the text. In one or two sentences, write what the book is about. _____

   _____

   _____

6. Read "Notes to the Students" if the text has one.

   What is the purpose of the text? _____

   What special features do the chapters have? _____

   What suggestions do(es) the author(s) give you? _____

   _____

   _____

7. Read the "Table of Contents." How many chapters does the text have? _____

8. Are the chapters grouped into units? _____

   If they are grouped into units, how many units does the text have? _____

9. Look at the chapters of each unit.

   How are they organized? _____

   Does each chapter explain its focus at the beginning? _____

10. On what page do you find the Index? _____

11. Does the text have a Glossary? If so, on what page do you find it? _____

12. On what page do you find the Appendix? _____

13. Is the Appendix general (only one section) or specific (two or more sections)? _____

14. If the Appendix is specific, what are the topics? _____

   _____

15. Does the text have a Bibliography? _____

16. Does the text have an Answer Key? _____

17. Does the text have Web support? _____ If so, what is the Web address? _____

   _____

18. Does the text have an accompanying floppy disk or CD-ROM? _____

Exercise 1.2

Directions: Use a chapter from one of your textbooks to complete the worksheet below.

1. Write the title of the chapter, then write one or two things you know about this topic.

   _____

   _____

2. Write the subheading of the chapter, then write one or two things you already know about each.

   _____

   _____

   _____

   _____

   _____

3. Read the chapter's objectives. In your own words, write what main points the chapter will cover.

   _____

   _____

   _____

   _____

   _____

4. Look at any pictures, charts, and/or graphs, then read the captions. How do they match with the objectives, title, and headers?

   _____

   _____

   _____

   _____

   _____

5. Are boldface and italics used? _____

6. Does the chapter have margin notes or chapter glossaries? _____

7. Is there a summary at the end of the chapter? _____

CHAPTER 2

Reading and Studying a Textbook

1. While Reading
  1.1 Purpose
  1.2 Titles into Questions
  1.3 Highlight Words
  1.4 Write Margin Notes
  1.5 Outline the Chapter
  1.6 Ask Questions
  1.7 Change Pace
  1.8 Reread

2. After Reading
  2.1 Reflect
  2.2 Look Over Notes
  2.3 Summarize
  2.4 Think

1. WHILE READING

Reading is a creative activity. Many ideas and questions go through your mind when reading. By previewing the material before actually reading a chapter, your mind will be more focused, thus increasing your concentration and retention of the material. However, there will still be times when the text can be challenging. By following these steps, you will be able to lessen, or hopefully eliminate, any confusion. Moreover, these steps will also help you prepare for what will happen after you finish reading the chapter: studying for the test.

1.1 Purpose

Establish a purpose for reading a text. Decide whether you are reading for a general understanding or a specific understanding of the information. If you are reading a chapter for a general understanding, you will need to ask yourself questions, highlight text, take margin and chapter notes, and summarize (discussed below). Also consider how this chapter ties in with class lectures and discussions. If you are reading for specific information, you might read only one part of a chapter. The way in which you read will change according to your purpose.

1.2 Titles into Questions

If you haven't already done so while previewing, change the titles in the headers into questions. As stated earlier, you will find the answers while reading. The following is an example of a chapter about statistical probability:

EXAMPLE: TURNING TITLES INTO QUESTIONS

Chapter Title: "Probability"
  Question: What is meant by probability?

Headers: "Fundamentals"
       "Subjective Probabilities"
       "Odds"
  Questions: What are the fundamentals of probability?
      What are subjective probabilities? How do these probabilities relate to the fundamentals of probability?
      What does the author mean by the odds of probability?

1.3 Highlight Words

After reading a paragraph or section, go back and highlight or underline any boldfaced or italicized words and their definitions, main ideas, examples, and key points made in the text. Be careful not to highlight too much or you will not be able to pinpoint the important information when reviewing the material. Draw a box around important vocabulary words (see Example 2.1).

1.4 Write Margin Notes

Write notes on what you read in the margins or on a separate piece of paper. (There are no fixed rules on how your notes should look—you can develop your own style.) Number important sequences of ideas. A margin note can simply be one word or an abbreviation of a key word, a short summary phrase, questions about the material, marking ideas you disagree with, or marking ideas that relate to something you have already read.

1.5 Outline the Chapter

Outline what you are reading. This will aid you while reviewing for a test. By using chapter notes, you will not have to reread the entire chapter before a test because all of the main ideas are in a shortened form. There are two styles of note taking that you can use: a traditional outline or a cluster. Either way provides you with a shortened form of the chapter's main ideas.

1.6 Ask Questions

Ask yourself questions about the text to clarify what you are reading.

1.7 Change Pace

Change your reading pace depending on the difficulty of the material. If you are familiar with or understand the subject or topic, then you could read at a faster pace. If you are reading unfamiliar or complicated material, then you would need to read more slowly.

1.8 Reread

Reread parts that you don't understand. Very few people are able to understand everything they read the first time through. Rereading makes learning easier; with practice, this technique will soon become a habit. You will eventually devise your own shortcuts for marking your text that will help you progress more swiftly. You will also discover that your reading comprehension and study skills are improving.

EXAMPLE 2.1 An Annotated (or Marked) Text

The following example shows how a reader annotated some pages.

PERSUASIVE WRITING

What is persuasive writing?
1. to get something you want
2. to get someone to accept your point of view
3. to get someone to do something.

Most writing is persuasive writing.

When you write, you want something. You want people to be more informed and to accept your point of view. You want them to do something. You want them to see you in a positive way. Good writing is writing that gets the effect you want.

A study of the techniques of persuasion will make you more concerned about your audience and about forms of writing that have a good or bad effect on them. It will keep you from speculating vaguely on some topic that cannot be proven with evidence. It will help you know when you are making sense.

How do you win your audience?
1. know your audience

Win Your Audience

To make a persuasive case, you have to know your audience. This will help you choose your words and shape your style.

One body of readers—say, a group of fraternity men—may respond to a direct appeal in strong language; another group—say, members of a Methodist congregation—may reject your whole argument if you use a word like "crap." One group will respond to wit, another to biblical quotations, and still another to a spread of statistics. Some readers will be offended if you write "Ms.," "ain't," "black," "symbiotic," "Dear Sir," or "and/or." Most audiences will be bored if you write vaguely about "Civic Responsibility" or "Tomorrow's Promise," but some audiences and occasions may call for rhetorical generalities. A detailed analysis of a social problem would be out of place at a political rally. The writing that would produce a great letter or advertisement might be unsuccessful in a sociology term paper. Some people will be impressed by "symbiotic relationships" and "a thousand points of light"; some won't. You have to know your audience.

2. create a personal voice by using a concerned and courteous tone.

A central feature in argument is creating a personal voice to express your views. Too often individuals with a strong case fail to be persuasive because their writing style makes them sound like a computer, a demanding top sergeant, a condescending aristocrat, or a stubborn child.   *MJ*

ex. of tone —→

Let your writing sound like a human voice. Most readers respond favorably to a concerned and courteous tone. When addressing a committee, refer to the members in your presentation. ("I'm sure you ladies and gentlemen recognize how complex this question is.") When writing a business letter, try to use a direct, personal style. ("I'm sorry about your problem, Mr. Baker, and I hope we can do more for you next time.") Routinely, work to avoid a hostile tone. Don't write, "You must do this," when you can say, "We would like you to do this promptly" or "I need this by Wednesday." Never write, "I will not do this," when you can say, "For these reasons, I cannot do this now." Don't protest, "You're too ignorant to understand my point"; say, "I am sorry I did not make myself understood."

This tone can be difficult to maintain. At times you will want to rage out with righteous indignation or ego-gratifying scorn. Don't do it. Remember that anger never persuaded anyone. In argument, nice guys finish first.

The point deserves repetition. An Alabama attorney looking back on a lifetime of courtroom experience said, "When I was young, I thought that lawyers won cases. Later I believed that facts won cases. Now I think that clients win cases. When the facts aren't overwhelmingly against him, the jury will find for the person they like best." The celebrated trails of Jean Harris, Larry Flint, John Delorean, Bernhard Goetz, and Jeffrey Dahmer seemed to work on that principle.

The persuasive force of sweet good-nature can hardly be overstated. Occasionally, lawyers have to press a personal injury suit against Disneyland or Walt Disney World. The attempts fail because Disney is too fixed in the public mind as sweet, clean, and moral. One frustrated lawyer said, "You might as well try to sue Mother Teresa."

How do you define the issue?
1. define the important terms

Define the Issue

A study of logic shows the importance of defining your issue. Some topics are flatly unarguable. They would produce vague speeches and incoherent essays.   *MJ*

Some issues rely more on a definition of terms than on evidence. When   *MJ* two people argue about whether Vice President Al Gore is handsome, for example, they are not disagreeing about his hair, teeth, or clothes, but about a definition of *handsomeness*. If they can agree on a definition, they will probably agree about Al Gore as well. Similarly, the question of whether capital punishment is wrong hinges not so much on the character of the act (the pain, the possibility of error, the protection afforded society) as on the definition or *wrongness*.

2. use objective standards

Aesthetic and moral questions are often unarguable because individuals *MJ* cannot agree on the terms involved. The meaning of any word is what a body of people say it is. (A telephone is called a *telephone* because English speakers regularly use that word to denote it.) But in these special areas, people do not agree. What is handsomeness? What is beauty? Theoreticians have sought objective standards, but the quest seems fruitless. Is a Greek temple more beautiful than a Gothic cathedral? Is Bach's music better than Madonna's? Who can say? The decision rests on a subjective judgment that does not lend itself to evidence. When friends tell you they prefer Smashing Pumpkins' music and the taste of Miller Lite, you can't argue with them. It's a good time to change the subject.

def. objective standards

using facts and evidence, not personal feelings or prejudices to judge something

def. subjective judgment

beliefs you believe to be true based on personal feeling or experiences

Like beauty, the idea of goodness is not easy to define. Seeking an objective basis for calling actions right and wrong, authorities have cited scriptural precedents; they have based systems on the inalienable rights of each human being; they have insisted that nature provides a moral example. But these definitions have not been universally accepted. If two individuals could agree that morality resides, say, in a natural law, they might then *begin* to talk about capital punishment. In general usage, however, moral terms remain so ill-defined that such issues cannot be argued meaningfully at all. (If you have to write on beauty or morality, focus your essay on some concrete example—say, arson or pop art or Vanna White—and work in as many "for example" and "for instance" references as you can.)

moral terms cannot be argued meaningfully

Moral and aesthetic questions are further removed from argument because they often produce emotional responses. Two individuals who agree in defining *handsomeness* might, for example, still disagree about former Vice President Gore because one objects to his liberal politics or his personal style. It is, of course, unreasonable to let emotions color such a judgment, but it happens all the time. You might be completely persuaded that capital punishment is cruel and barbaric yet, at a given moment, argue that hanging is too good for a child murderer or a political terrorist.

3. make your definitions specific, not vague

Vague definitions make an argument in many areas. Saab has been proclaimed "the most *intelligent* car ever built," and Royal Copenhagen "the only *elegant* musk oil cologne." The advertisement insists "Only Tareyton has the *best* filter!" Are these claims true? Until the key words are defined, the statements are no more subject to being proved with evidence than is "Razzle dragons, popple stix." Nonsense is neither true nor false.

Many areas of modern controversy hinge on definitions of terms. Do animals "talk"? Can children "sin"? Is running a "religious" experience? Is prostitution a "victimless" crime? Do computers "think"? It depends on how you define the words.

Terms must be defined and accepted before you can prove something.

Only when terms are defined and mutually accepted can you begin gathering evidence to prove something. You can, for example, argue whether

> Jim Brown or Walter Payton was the better football player because their records, the merits of their supporting and opposing teams, and the qualities of a good running back are generally agreed on. Is it true that smoking causes lung cancer, that former President Clinton knew about the details of the Whitewater scandal, that Gordon's is the largest-selling gin in the world? These questions can at least be argued.

Source: Daniel McDonald and Larry W. Burton. *The Language of Argument,* Ninth Edition. Copyright © 1999 by Longman Publishers. Reprinted by permission of Pearson Education, Inc.

2. AFTER READING

Often when students finish reading a chapter, they immediately close the book and do something else. Wait! You read a chapter to learn a specific process, concept, or idea, and you may feel confident in your understanding of what you have read. However, you will eventually be tested on the material, probably several days or weeks after reading the chapter. By that time, you may have forgotten what you read. By following these steps, you will be able to increase your retention of what you learned and be organized for future study.

2.1 Reflect

Reflect on what you have just read. At this point, the information is in your short-term memory. Therefore, ask yourself what the chapter was about and then answer this question as completely as possible. This helps to reinforce what you have read.

2.2 Look Over Notes

Look over any chapter notes that you have written. Rewrite anything that is not clear.

2.3 Summarize

Write a short summary that includes the main points of the chapter.

2.4 Think

Think about how this chapter relates to the chapters you have already read and to what the instructor is discussing in class.

Exercises

1. Directions: Look back at Example 2.1 (pp. 9–12). Write an outline and general summary using the highlighted portions and the margin notes.
2. Select a chapter from one of the texts you are using in another class and annotate, outline, and summarize it.
3. On a piece of paper, write down any abbreviations or annotations that you use to take notes. Compare yours to those of other members of the class. Write down any new ones that you think will be helpful for you in the future.

Discussion Questions

1. How can previewing help you become a better and more focused reader?
2. How can summarizing and outlining a chapter help you more effectively study for a test?

CHAPTER 3

Lectures and Note Taking

1. Lecture Notes	2. Note-Taking Methods

1. LECTURE NOTES

Very few students can remember everything that an instructor has said over the course of a semester. Therefore, the ability to take good notes is an essential skill that every college student should possess. Besides helping you to remember what was said in the lecture, note taking also helps you to concentrate in class. Your notes are also clues to ideas and information that your instructor thinks are important. These ideas will probably appear on a test or show up in an assignment. There are a variety of note-taking methods that you could use, but by following the suggestions below, you can devise a system that best fits your needs.

2. NOTE-TAKING METHODS

- **Write the class name and date at the top of the page.**
- **Write in outline form, not in essay form.** Unless you know shorthand, you will not be able to write down every word that the instructor says.
- **Listen for main ideas and key points.** By concentrating on writing the details, you may miss an important main idea. Listen for points that the instructor emphasizes.
- **Write your notes in your own words.** Don't worry about spelling, grammar, punctuation, or the like. Just get the information down on paper.
- **Listen for key transition words.** Listen especially for words such as *first, second, next,* and *finally.* These transitions indicate that the instructor is moving from point to point.
- **Develop your own abbreviation code.** For example: w/o (without), b/c (because), ex (for example). Remember to be consistent with your abbreviations. (See Example 3.1, page 14.)
- **Ask questions to clarify ideas that you don't understand.** Most instructors welcome thoughtful questions.
- **Underline key words or points** in your notes and text.
- **Write down what the instructor writes on the board or overhead.**
- **Read the material from the text before class if possible.** By doing this, the lecture will be more comprehensible and your notes will be better. Most instructors assume that you've read the material before class.
- **Read over and rewrite your notes as soon as possible after the class.** Add any details or examples from the text. Naturally, the sooner you do this, the more details and examples you will remember. This will be very helpful when studying for tests, and so on.
- **Ask to copy another student's notes if you must miss class.** However, it is always better to attend class.
- **Keep your notes in a binder organized by date and subject.** If your notes are thrown into your book bag or textbook after class, you may not be able to find them when it's time to study.
- **Ask your instructors if they have their own Web sites.** Instructors often post their lecture notes.

The most important thing to remember is to listen carefully and be consistent with your note taking. With effort and practice, your note-taking skills will improve and taking good notes will become easier.

Example 3.1 Shorthand Annotations for Note Taking

The following is an example of the type of annotation you can use when writing margin notes.

=	equals	c.f.	compare
≠	not equal	e.g.	for example
∴	therefore	#	number
b/c	because	etc.	(et cetera) and so on
&, +	and	def.	definition
>	more than	nec.	necessary
<	less than	w/	with
→	causes, produces	w/o	without
i.e.	that is	MI	main idea

Exercises

1. Directions: Get a binder, dividers, and clean notebook paper. Label and use your dividers to separate the binder into sections for each class, for example, Math 1, English 2, Biology 3, and Speech 4. At the beginning of each section, place the course outline (syllabus) that your instructor gave you on the first day of class. After that, include plenty of notebook paper for taking notes. At the end of the section, place any handouts that the instructor has given you.

2. On a piece of paper, write down any abbreviations or annotations that you use to take notes. Compare yours to those of other members of the class. Write down any new ones that you think will be helpful for you in the future.

CHAPTER 4

Participating in Class

1. Participation Suggestions

In many countries, a good student is considered to be one who sits quietly, listens attentively, takes good notes, and doesn't question the instructor or fellow students. The American educational system is quite different. Of course, instructors like students who are attentive and are good note takers, but they also expect students to ask questions and challenge what they hear. If working in groups, they expect students to be actively engaged in discussions with one another. Instructors tend to perceive students who participate in class discussions as being motivated and knowledgeable—an important perception when giving grades. Class participation helps you to concentrate and stay focused during class. Therefore, it is important to actively participate in class. To become more active in class, try the following suggestions.

1. PARTICIPATION SUGGESTIONS

- **Be prepared for class.** This includes reading the text or completing any activity that was assigned prior to class.
- **Have several comments and/or questions ready before class.**
- **Make your comments short and to the point.**
- **Listen carefully to other students' comments.** Respect their opinions and try to understand them.
- **Base your comments on what you learned from the text or other related sources as well as your own experiences.** In other words, don't base your comments on how you feel at that moment.

Developing good participation skills is not only essential for college, but it is an important skill you will use later on in your career.

Discussion

In a group, discuss the different ways that you prepare for class.

CHAPTER 5
Collaborative Learning

1. Peer Critique
   1.1 Preparation
   1.2 Read the Draft
   1.3 Comment on Strengths
   1.4 Comment on Weaknesses

2. Group Work and Projects
   2.1 Collaborative Learning Suggestions

1. PEER CRITIQUE

Collaborative learning takes many forms. One of the most useful is peer critique, which involves having students evaluate each other's work. This technique can be used for many different kinds of assignments, but in college it is most often used for written work. Using peer critique, students read and comment on each other's written drafts. The idea is to evaluate the draft and then make helpful suggestions on how to improve it.

1.1 Preparation

Prepare to make your comments by either writing on the draft or on a separate sheet of paper. Writing directly on the draft has some advantages because the author can easily see where you've made marks in the text and comments in the margins. However, some people prefer not to have their drafts marked on, so ask ahead of time and use a separate sheet if the author doesn't want you to write on the draft. Also, some instructors hand out peer critique forms for students to complete. Peer critique methods vary, so follow your instructor's preferences.

1.2 Read the Draft

Read the draft carefully and thoroughly, twice if time permits. Check to see if the author followed the assignment and guidelines given. This is the first and primary consideration.

1.3 Comment on Strengths

Unless you are instructed otherwise, begin by commenting on what the author did well, what is good about the writing, and anything else you liked. Perhaps the author used a great example to make a point, or the writing style is smooth and flowing, or the author used humor very well. Comment on the strengths in the draft.

1.4 Comment on Weaknesses

Lastly, comment on things that need to be improved and mark or note any errors that need correcting. Perhaps the introduction is poorly written, or the thesis is unclear, or the information drifts off topic halfway through the paper. Note your concern and make a suggestion for improvement, if you have one. Also mark any errors you notice that need correcting, such as spelling, grammar, or punctuation problems. However, these are things to be taken care of during proofreading, so don't dwell on them. Make comments only if you see repeated errors in word usage, run-on sentences, or misused commas, etc. It's okay if you are not expert at spelling, grammar, or punctuation—just comment on what you do know and make as many helpful suggestions as you can. Concentrate on the content of the paper and what improvements are needed to strengthen it.

2. GROUP WORK AND PROJECTS

Often an instructor will assign projects that require students to work in groups. Increasingly, college classes are requiring collaborative learning and group projects from students. Linked classes and collaborative learning "teams" are becoming common on many campuses. Some students do not like group work because they feel that some members of the group may not contribute equally or may not carry through with their part of the assignment, or they may find some group members to be argumentative. However, group work skills are important to learn, and if groups work well together,·the advantages to working in groups outweigh the disadvantages.

First, groups allow you to learn more because they can generate a greater quantity and quality of ideas—remember, many heads are better than one. Next, because of the number of ideas generated, students learn the subject matter in greater depth. Finally, working together in a group is an essential skill that must be learned not only for college but for the workplace as well. There are very few jobs that allow you to work independently from others. Employers value employees with good collaborative working skills. The following suggestions will help your group work together successfully.

2.1 Collaborative Learning Suggestions

- *Divide the work as evenly as possible* so that no one in the group will feel that they are carrying too much of the workload.

- *Make a time line for the stages of the project* so that everyone in the group is clear as to when their part of the project is due. Make sure the schedule is flexible enough to handle any unforeseen problems that may arise.

- *Be honest about your capabilities.* Do not volunteer to do a part of the assignment that you know that you cannot do.

- *Listen actively.* Your body language should show that you are listening to what others are saying. This means making eye contact and nodding your head.

- *Ask questions for clarification.* Write down words or ideas to help you remember what was said for further discussion, and summarize or comment on what you have heard.

- *Interrupt tactfully and politely.* Even though it is considered impolite to interrupt, there might come a point when it is necessary. Therefore, if you must interrupt, do so when the speaker has finished with his or her sentence or idea, and be polite. For example, say, "Excuse me, Frank, but I would like to add something to that when you are finished." Or "Excuse me, Jeannie. I am confused by your last comment. Could you explain it again?"

- *Reply to interruptions politely.* If you are interrupted without a good reason, respond in a firm yet friendly tone of voice, for example, "Please let me finish making my point."

- *Compliment good ideas.* Be gracious concerning the contributions of others.

- *Learn how to disagree by challenging the ideas, not the person.* Never use put-downs during a discussion. It is okay to politely challenge a point someone makes or that person's information or source. It is not okay to make personal comments or attacks. Verbally attacking a member of the group is the fastest way to destroy the group's cohesion. Don't say, "Debbie, don't be such an idiot." Instead say, "Debbie, I'm not sure that your ideas will work." You could also ask a few questions about important points that may have been missed. For example, say, "That might work, but did you think about. . . ."

Working well in groups simply involves showing respect and common courtesy to others and it teaches skills that people use throughout their lives.

Exercise 5.1

Class Exercise: Peer Review

Directions: Trade essays with another student in your class. Then read through the form below to focus on what to review. Next, read the entire essay before you write any comments. Finally, fill in the form.

Date _____

Class _____

Author _____

Peer Reviewer _____

Introduction

1. Does the title reflect the main point of the essay? Y/N

2. Write the thesis statement. Circle the topic and underline the controlling idea(s).

    _____

    _____

3. Does the thesis clearly state what the essay will be about? Y/N

4. Does the introduction contain background information that is relevant to the thesis? Y/N

Body

5. Do each of the paragraphs support the thesis? Y/N
    If no, which paragraphs do not?

    _____

6. Does each paragraph have a clearly stated topic? Y/N
    If no, which paragraphs do not?

    _____

7. Do each of the paragraphs provide enough concrete support for the topic? Y/N
    If no, which paragraphs do not?

    _____

8. Does the author use transitions to connect ideas between and within each paragraph? Y/N
    If no, which paragraphs need transitions?

    _____

Conclusion

9. Does the conclusion clearly restate the thesis? Y/N

10. Does the conclusion summarize the main points of the essay? Y/N

11. Does the essay end with an appropriate concluding remark? Y/N

Further Feedback

12. Write two or more strengths of the essay.

    _____

    _____

_____

_____

_____

_____

13. Write two or more suggestions that would improve the essay. (Use the form to help.) Be as specific as possible.

_____

_____

_____

_____

_____

_____

_____

Discussion Questions

    1. What are the strengths and weaknesses when working in groups?
    2. What are the strengths and weaknesses of peer review exercises?

CHAPTER 6

Test Taking

1. Types of Tests
   1.1 Objective Tests
       1.1.1 Multiple Choice
       1.1.2 True/False
       1.1.3 Matching
   1.2 Essay Tests
2. Test Preparation
   2.1 Know the Test Schedule
   2.2 Ask Questions
   2.3 Schedule Study Time
   2.4 Organize Study Material
   2.5 Develop a Study Plan
   2.6 Rest and Nourishment

3. Taking the Test
   3.1 Test Time
   3.2 Listen
   3.3 List Information
   3.4 Check Your Answers
   3.5 Read the Directions
   3.6 Answer the Easy Questions First
   3.7 Leave Enough Time
   3.8 Write Neatly
   3.9 Double Check

Too often, students start studying for a test a night or two before the day the test takes place. If the test is a comprehensive midterm or final, it may involve several chapters of the text as well as all of the lecture notes taken during the course. If your notes from the text and lectures are unorganized or vague and you have not given yourself time to adequately prepare, this will increase any anxiety that you naturally have before a test and, more important, decrease your chances for doing well on the test. Therefore, in order to do well on a test, you must be organized and well-prepared.

1. TYPES OF TESTS

In college, there are several types of tests that you will likely encounter.

1.1 Objective Tests

Objective tests come in three varieties: multiple choice, true/false, and matching. By the time you reach college, you are probably familiar with these formats. However, if you are an international student, these tests may come as a surprise because many countries use only essay-type tests.

1.1.1 *Multiple Choice*

In a multiple-choice test, you have several answers from which to choose. When taking this type of test, read the directions carefully. You may be asked to mark the correct answer, the best answer, or all of the answers that are correct. Read all of the answers before you mark the one that you think is correct.

1.1.2 *True/False*

You have two answer choices in this test: true or false. Read the entire statement before you answer. Sometimes the first part of the statement is true but the second part is false. *All* of the statement must be true for the answer to be true. Often statements are false if they contain words such as *all, every, never,* and so on. Pay special attention to statements that contain negatives. Remember, a negative statement that is correct is true; for example, "The world is not flat."

1.1.3 *Matching*

When taking a matching test, read both lists completely before you begin answering. Cross out each answer as you find its match, unless you are told not to mark on the test. Match word-to-word answers according to their parts of speech, for example, a noun to a noun. Match words to a phrase by first reading the phrase and then looking for the word that describes it. Use capital letters because they are easier to read.

1.2 Essay Tests

Another common test you will encounter is the essay test. This is the type of test many students dread. If you have a strategy and follow it, you will have greater success when taking this type of test.

Read and reread the prompt or question until you are sure of what the instructor is asking you to do. Look for key words, for example, *contrast, compare, define,* or *explain the effects of.* If you contrast instead of compare as the instructor requested, your answer is wrong no matter how well-written your essay is. Next, rephrase the question into a thesis, for example:

> *Prompt:* Explain three effects that the war in Vietnam had on the United States.
> *Thesis:* "The Vietnam War had three major effects on the United States."

Write a quick outline to organize your thoughts. Finally, allow enough time at the end of the test to edit and proofread your work.

2. TEST PREPARATION

As stated above, if you have not given yourself enough time to prepare for an exam, you will most likely experience increased anxiety, which usually results in lower test scores. Following the guidelines below will help you be more successful in taking tests.

2.1 Know the Test Schedule

Look at your course outline. Most instructors will list the dates for major exams.

2.2 Ask Questions

Clarify with your instructor what will be covered on the test and what type of questions will be asked on the test (e.g., true/false, multiple choice, essay).

2.3 Schedule Study Time

Schedule the times and places that you will study and stick to that schedule.

2.4 Organize Study Material

Organize your notes from your text and lectures. Make sure you know which chapters from the text will be covered on the test.

2.5 Develop a Study Plan

As you develop a study time schedule, plan what you will study and stick to it. For example, you might decide to study the first two chapters that will be covered on the test and the notes that relate to those chapters on Monday, the next two chapters and notes on Tuesday, the next two on Wednesday, and the day before the test, review the areas that are giving you trouble.

2.6 Rest and Nourishment

Get plenty of sleep and enough to eat before the test.

3. TAKING THE TEST

Most people are nervous the day of a test. Not only is this to be expected, but a little bit of nervousness may help you to be more mentally alert. However, don't let nerves interfere with your test taking. Try to stay calm and focused. Follow the tips on the next page and you will do fine.

3.1 Test Time

Get to class ahead of time. Rushing in at the last minute will only cause heightened anxiety.

3.2 Listen

Listen carefully to the instructor's directions before the test. Ask questions to clarify any part that you don't understand.

3.3 List Information

Put your name, date, and any other information your instructor wants on the test.

3.4 Check Your Answers

Look over the test to note the number of sections, the types of questions asked, and the point value for the questions. This will tell you which questions are most important to answer, and it will enable you to gauge your time accordingly to make sure you finish the test.

3.5 Read the Directions

Make sure to do so for each section. Although you see that a section is multiple choice, the directions might say "Choose the correct answer," or "Choose the correct answers."

3.6 Answer the Easy Questions First

If you linger too long on some questions, you may not finish the test. Also, the other questions on the test may help you answer the questions you are unsure of.

3.7 Leave Enough Time

Pace yourself and leave enough time at the end of the session to look over the test and check your answers.

3.8 Write Neatly

Instructors will not give you credit for answers that they cannot read.

3.9 Double Check

Make sure that the number of the question and the answer number match if you are using a Scantron® or other fill-in-the-bubble test forms.

Following these time-tested suggestions and techniques will help you to be better prepared and to score better on your tests. It's worthwhile to practice and master as many of these suggestions and techniques as possible.

Discussion Question

In a group, discuss how you will prepare for your next test.

CHAPTER 7
Writing College Essays and Papers

1. Planning (Prewriting)
   1.1 Think About Your Topic
   1.2 Gather Information
   1.3 Develop a Thesis
   1.4 Know Your Purpose
   1.5 Consider Your Audience
   1.6 Organize Your Information
       1.6.1 Edit the Information
       1.6.2 Group Related Information
       1.6.3 Outline Your Ideas

2. Writing
   2.1 Write a Draft
   2.2 Revise Your Draft
   2.3 Format Your Draft
   2.4 Proofread and Compose the Final Draft

1. PLANNING (PREWRITING)

Good planning and preparation are the keys to good writing.

1.1 Think About Your Topic

Good writing starts with clear thinking. Those who learn to write well know that a good deal of thinking needs to take place before any writing happens. Many people who have trouble writing have this trouble because they don't know how to get started. A writer needs to start by thinking about the topic. Usually, in college or professional life, the topic is given, at least in a general way. For example, you may be assigned to write about sexual harassment policy or write a position paper about censorship on the Internet.

Start by thinking about the topic. Let your mind focus on it. Ask yourself: What do I already know about the topic? What do I not know? What do I need to know?

1.2 Gather Information

Begin by brainstorming and perhaps jotting down information and ideas. Let your mind flow with the topic. Don't concern yourself with what the information or ideas are; just write down anything that occurs to you that is related to the topic. If it helps to make mind maps or to use other graphics or to make lists, then do so. Brainstorm until you can't think of anything else to jot down. Be as specific as possible with any details, such as names, places, dates, descriptions, and so on.

After you've finished brainstorming, look back at the information and ideas you've thought of and written down. Review the material to see if anything else occurs to you. Think about what other information you might need to gather. What else do you need to know? What questions might someone have about your information? Make a note or two about where you think you could find the information you still need. If you need to go to other sources, such as the library, the Internet, or databases to get information and do some research, then do so. Make copies of the information, mark it up, highlight passages, etc.

When you've gathered all the information you think you'll need, stop and double check. You need a lot of information and details to work with, of course, but make sure that you have the most basic information: the five Ws + H. Do you have all of the information for your topic regarding who, what, where, when, why, and how? Do you have names and specific details? If you discover that you are missing any information or necessary details, go back to your sources and get them. It is important to have all of your information beforehand. It facilitates the planning and prevents many writing problems.

1.3 Develop a Thesis

You need to know the thesis of your paper before you try to write the paper. In grade school, we're taught that a paper's thesis is its main idea. This is true, but what *is* the main idea? Writers think of a thesis in somewhat more precise terms. A thesis should contain two pieces of information: the topic and your position or opinion. You should be able to state your thesis in one sentence. For example: "The Internet should not be censored." The topic is "The Internet," and your position/opinion is ". . . should not be censored." Write your thesis statement in your notes and information. You can modify it later if necessary, but for now decide what it will be and write it down. Knowing your thesis helps you to determine the direction you are going to take with your information when you write your paper, report, etc.

1.4 Know Your Purpose

Take another moment and consider your purpose. What are you trying to accomplish by communicating the information you will be writing? Are you simply trying to give information that was requested, or are you also attempting to explain the information? Do you need to convince your audience to see it your way? Whatever your purpose, you should write it down in one sentence, just as you did for your thesis. For example, "The purpose of my paper is *to convince* readers that the Internet should not be censored." Refer to your thesis to help you compose your purpose statement. You can modify it later, if necessary, but write it down as best as you can for now. Knowing your purpose ahead of time gives you focus. It helps you to tailor your information and presentation to fit your thesis and audience.

Another reason it is good to know your purpose ahead of time is that it allows you to know when you are done with your paper. Some writers have trouble knowing when to stop writing. When you have fulfilled your purpose, you're done. If you've planned carefully, this usually coincides with discovering that you've used all of your information.

1.5 Consider Your Audience

Take a few moments to consider who your audience will be. Who is going to be reading this paper? What do your readers already know about the topic, if anything? What do they need to know?

Also consider what you know about your readers. What level of education do they have? What field is their specialty? What about differences in age, gender, and so on? What about cultural differences? The answers to these questions will affect the approach you take and the tone of your paper.

Considering your audience will help you to mentally set a language level for writing your paper. Your mind will start working on choosing the right words and phrasing for what you are going to tell the readers. It will also help alert you to special considerations you might have to take into account when communicating to others, especially if topic familiarity or cultural differences are factors.

1.6 Organize Your Information

It is better and easier to organize your information and material *before* you write rather than to try to do it after you've made a draft. Making yourself understood is the most important thing in communication and requires careful thought and organization. Organization has three substeps: editing, grouping, and outlining.

1.6.1 *Edit the Information*

You may wonder what there is to edit since you haven't written your paper yet. At this point in the process, it is your information that needs editing. Discard any information you don't need and keep only what you will need. How do you know the difference? Look at your thesis and purpose. Keep whatever information will support your thesis and fulfill your purpose. Toss out the rest. If you're not sure about a piece of information, keep it for now. You can toss it later if you don't use it.

1.6.2 *Group Related Information*

Take the information you've kept and sort it into groups. Base these groups on related information. For example: This information is about free speech; it goes together into a group. This information is about Internet access; it is another group. This is about filtering software; it's a group . . . and so on. Make sure that each piece of information you have is put in the appropriate group. If it helps to circle information, make lists or partial paragraphs, or draw information/subject trees, then do so. You may want to name or title your groups to remember and identify what's in them.

1.6.3 *Outline Your Ideas*

This step does not have to be difficult. In the past it has been difficult for many writers, who may have developed a habit of skipping it. Don't! Outlining is not a big problem if it is done properly. Most people were introduced in grade school to outlines like the one on the left. Writers rarely use this format and then only for projects that are very lengthy or complex, such as books or government proposals. Most writing does not require this; a scratch outline is sufficient for most projects. See the example on the right.

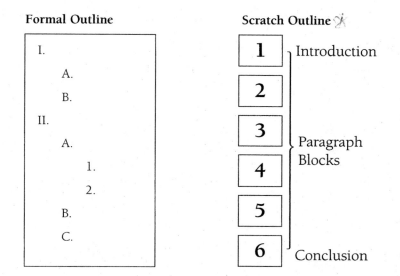

Simply decide in what order to put your groups of information. What do you have to tell first? Then what? What should the reader know after that? Just number the groups of information in order and stack them up like blocks: 1, 2, 3, 4. . . . Don't forget to put an Introduction at the beginning and a Conclusion at the end. You're done. That's an outline. It should tell you the order in which you are going to present your information. That's about all it has to do, and it can double as the table of contents if necessary.

2. WRITING

2.1 Write a Draft

Only now do you write, and writing should be easier and even faster because all you have to do is transcribe the information from your groups of information into sentences and paragraphs in the order you decided on when you organized the information. While you are writing your draft, do not concern yourself with spelling or grammar or mechanics; just write out the information as you've planned. Don't worry about the introduction or labor over your wording at this time. Keep on track and let the information flow as best as you can. Other considerations will only disrupt or break your concentration, and they are not important yet. Your goal for now is to simply get it all down on paper or into the computer. Even if it takes a while, finish the draft before you go on to the next step in the writing process. Don't worry about what it looks like, as long as you can read it.

2.2 Revise Your Draft

After you have finished writing your draft, you will need to revise it (see Figure 7.1) to make sure your information is clear and complete, the ideas are well-presented, and the material is as readable and understandable as you can make it. Check the content to see that all necessary information is included. Check the organization to make sure everything ended up in the right place. If you need to rearrange material for clarity or to improve the flow or your reasoning or logic, then do so. Get input from others if you wish. Often others will see something you might have missed.

Rewrite as necessary, but don't let this become an endless task. Once you have said what you have to say as best you can say it, let that be the end of it. If you planned carefully and well, then the draft and the revision process should go well. If you run into a serious problem, backtrack through the planning process and correct it, then bring the process up to date, correct the problem, and finish your revisions.

Figure 7.1 Sample Revision of a Student Essay (Page 1)

Supporting the Arts *on Campus*

It's worthwhile to support the arts *on campus* and the most economical way is to purchase a~~n~~ *season* Arts Pass. An Arts Pass allows students into all ~~campus~~ *college* shows and performances. ~~for an entire semester.~~ Nowhere else can you get such a variety of entertainment for roughly the price of *one date at the* ~~two~~ movie*s* ~~tickets~~, and it's good all semester.

Consider the art shows, ~~the~~ music concerts, and ~~the~~ theatrical *and dance* performances ~~you could~~ *one can* enjoy each semester. Every department in the Fine and Performing Arts program sponsors numerous shows and performances on campus *over a dozen a semester.* Some are free to students, some charge a nominal fee, and a few charge for student tickets, but an Arts Pass gives admission to every arts ~~venue.~~ *event.*

This semester, for example, the Art Gallery will sponsor two ~~shows.~~ *exhibits.* The first is a showing by a group *of painters* from an art colony in Montery, and the second is the annual sp student Art Show, which will include this year's art competition winners in the drawing, painting, sculpting, ceramics, and mixed media categories. The Main Stage Theatre will have performances of Shakespeare's comedy *A Midsummer's Night Dream* and the sp musical *Caberet.* It will also host the Harlem Dance troupe and the annual Modern sp Dance Festival. The Recitall Hall is featuring a classic piano recitall and hosting the sp annual Cool Jazz Concert. ~~And there's more.~~ *These are but a few of what is being offered.*

2.3 Format Your Draft

Certain documents require specific formatting (margins, line spacing, paragraphing, etc.), such as college essays, research papers, memorandums, business letters, reports, and case study analyses. Determine the correct format for the paper you've written and arrange your information into that format. Check the examples in your texts or other professional sources and use the format they use. Pay close attention to the requirements and conventions of the format and make sure to follow them, including any necessary documentation. (See Part III: Basic Document Design and Format.)

2.4 Proofread and Compose Final Draft

The final stage of the writing process is to proofread for the final draft. At this stage, you are looking for errors in wording, grammar, spelling, punctuation, mechanics, etc. Read over your paper slowly, purposefully looking for mistakes, errors, typos, etc. Use dictionaries, spell checkers, and other tools to help you. Read the paper aloud. Often you can hear an error you might not see. This last step is very important because the way a document looks and reads is as much a part of the presentation as what it says. Take the time to do this carefully.

The final product will be presented to the reader(s) in printed or published form. It should be as error-free as possible. If you have followed all of the writing process steps in order, then you should have a paper you can be proud of and one that looks good as well.

Exercises

Write an essay on one of the following topics. Use the writing process to plan and prepare your paper. Complete each step as best you can as you move through the process.

1. Prepare and write an essay about a major decision that you've made in your life and how making that decision has affected your life. Some possible topics include: going to college, moving away from home, going into military service, getting married, having children, a major surgery, divorce, or change of career.

2. Decision making usually involves comparing and contrasting available choices. Prepare and write an essay comparing and contrasting two people, two places, or two objects. Make sure that the two topics you pick have enough in common to be fairly compared. Then, in your paper, be clear about which you prefer, if you have a preference, and why. Some possible topics include: two teachers, two actors, two friends, two restaurants, two vacation spots, two homes, two sports cars, two video games, or two different places you've worked.

3. Write an essay describing something you know how to do that you learned at home, at work, or from training that you've had. Write the essay clearly enough so that someone who was unfamiliar with the process could follow your instructions and get the correct results. Some possible topics include: painting a room, doing laundry, planting a garden, operating a particular computer program, running a cash register, working a grill, serving customers, taking someone's blood pressure, driving a forklift, or closing a store.

CHAPTER 8

Structuring College Essays and Papers

| 1. Introduction | 2. Body | 3. Conclusion |

1. INTRODUCTION

The thesis of your essay is usually stated somewhere in the first paragraph, the introductory paragraph. Your thesis should state the topic of your essay *and* indicate your position, opinion, or point of view on the topic. Keep your topic limited, specific, and focused. You should present definite and clear reasons to support your thesis. Provide any introductory or background information about your topic that your reader needs to know to understand what your essay is about and what you'll be discussing. (See Example 8.1.)

2. BODY

The first paragraph in the body of your essay should discuss your first reason or support point for your thesis. The first sentence in each paragraph should be your topic sentence, simply stating what the information in the paragraph is about. All other sentences in the paragraph should contain information to support the topic or make your point. Use specific examples, personal experience, data, statistics, or quotes to support your point.

The second paragraph in the body of your essay should state your second reason or support point for your thesis. It should be a smooth and logical transition from the previous paragraph. Remember to keep each paragraph focused on one piece of information, one reason, one topic. Support that topic with whatever information is appropriate, then move to the next paragraph.

The third paragraph in the body of your essay should give your third reason or support point for your thesis. Once again, make sure to support your topic sentence with specific examples, personal experience, data, or quotes, etc. Make certain that the information in the paragraph flows smoothly and logically from the preceding paragraphs and information.

Keep doing the same thing for all paragraphs. State the topic of the paragraph in the first sentence of each paragraph. Then support the topic with specific examples, personal experience, data, statistics, quotes, etc., until you've made your point, one paragraph at a time, and you've said everything you planned to say. You should put your strongest reason or support point in the last body paragraph because people tend to consider what they read at the end of a sentence, paragraph, or paper as the most important information.

3. CONCLUSION

The final paragraph, your concluding or summary paragraph, should recall your thesis and draw your essay to a conclusion. It might mention your reasons or strongest support points *briefly,* to reinforce them and to remind your reader of them. You may also suggest how your thesis can be applied to related or future situations. This writing pattern can be carried on indefinitely. It can be used to create a standard college essay or a twenty-page research paper or report by simply extending this writing pattern to as many paragraphs as is necessary to adequately cover the topic. With practice, you will be able to use this format to improve your writing more and more as time goes on.

Example 8.1 Sample Student Essay

Bennett 1

Identification Block

Amanda Bennett

Prof. Jane Wingo

English 102A

25 January 2003

Title

Introductory Paragraph

Supporting the Arts on Campus

It's worthwhile to support the arts on campus and the most economical way is to purchase a season Arts Pass. An Arts Pass allows students into all college shows and performances. Nowhere else can students get such a variety of entertainment for roughly the price of one date at the movies, and it's good all semester.

Body Paragraph #1

Consider the art shows, music concerts, and theatrical and dance performances one can enjoy each semester. Every department in the Fine and Performing Arts program sponsors numerous shows and performances on campus, over a dozen per semester. Some are free to students, some charge a nominal fee, and a few charge for student tickets, but an Arts Pass gives admission to every arts event.

Body Paragraph #2

This semester, for example, the Art Gallery will sponsor two exhibits. The first is a showing by a group of painters from an art colony in Monterey, and the second is the annual Student Art Show, which will include this year's art competition winners in the drawing, painting, sculpting, ceramics, and mixed media categories. The Main Stage Theatre will have performances of Shakespeare's comedy *A Midsummer Night's Dream* and the musical *Cabaret*. It will also host the Harlem Dance Troupe and the annual Modern Dance Festival. The Recital Hall is featuring a classic piano recital and hosting the annual Cool Jazz Concert. These are but a few examples of what is being offered.

Body Paragraph #3

However, shows and performances need to be seen. The dedication of the talented artists and performers, and their instructors and mentors, make the shows and performances possible, but it is our active participation that makes them thrive. Our patronage helps support the arts on campus and in the community at large. Part of the contribution made when purchasing a ticket or an Arts Pass goes to support scholarships for students majoring in fine and performing arts, pays honoraria and performance fees for guest artists to conduct master classes and workshops, and helps fund publication of *College Arts*.

Concluding Paragraph

When students are considering things to do and places to go during the semester, they should remember what is available on campus. The shows and performances are fun and entertaining, and a good value. Purchasing an Arts Pass is even better. Either way, becoming a patron of the arts will not only enrich the arts, it will enrich us as well.

Exercises

Write an essay on one of the following topics. Use the writing process to plan and prepare your paper. Complete each step as best you can as you move through the process.

1. Prepare and write an essay about something that you think should be made illegal (or remain legal). Support your argument with facts and logic. Some possible topics include: ACT/SAT testing, capital punishment, casino gambling, euthanasia, genetic engineering, human cloning, pornographic websites, racial profiling, racial preferences, smoking in public places, and stem cell research.

2. Write an essay describing someone or some place that holds special memories for you. Describe the person or place fully so that you draw a complete picture for the reader. Try to create a dominant (main) impression of the person or place.

3. College allows you to explore career choices. If you have made a career choice, write an essay explaining what led you to make that career choice. Include people, experiences, teachers, stories, films, classes you have taken, summer jobs; in short, any inspiration or influence that inspired you to make your choice.

CHAPTER 9

Writing Effective Paragraphs

1. Paragraphs	1.2 Supporting Information
1.1 Topic Sentence	1.3 Checking the Information

1. PARAGRAPHS

A paragraph is a unit of information or thought that supports a paper's thesis or main idea. When you organize your information, you group related information into blocks. These blocks usually become the paragraphs of your paper. These paragraphs have a standard structure: a topic sentence, and information that supports the topic sentence. You must also ensure that your facts in each paragraph are accurate and complete.

1.1 Topic Sentence

Begin each paragraph with a sentence that simply states what the paragraph is about, what information it contains. For example, if you are writing a paper opposing Internet censorship (your thesis), you may wish to point out that no one country has jurisdiction over what's posted on the Internet. That paragraph of your paper might begin: "The Internet is international and no single country or its laws can control the Internet." The topic sentence should always be the first sentence of the paragraph.

1.2 Supporting Information

Each topic sentence should be followed by information that supports whatever the topic sentence states or claims. This information can be in the form of an example, research data, a quote from an expert, or some fact. Whatever the information is, it supports the topic sentence by providing an example, giving a reason, or clarifying the point you are making by providing detailed information. These detailed examples, facts, quotes, and so on were collected during the Gathering Information step of the writing process, and now you are using them. (See Chapter 7.)

1.3 Checking the Information

During the revision step of the writing process, check the information in each paragraph. First, make sure that the information does what it is supposed to do: Does the information clearly relate to and support the topic sentence? If not, revise the information (and the topic sentence, if necessary) so that the topic and related information are clearly tied together as a unit.

Second, make certain that the information is sufficient and strong enough to support the topic of the paragraph. Do you need to expand on your example or add to the facts you've provided to make your point stronger or more clear? If so, revise and add in additional details.

Finally, check your language flow and style. Do your sentences flow together, one to another, and are the information and ideas clearly related to each other within the paragraph? If necessary, rewrite sentences to achieve better clarity and flow.

Paragraphs grow naturally from the Organization steps of the writing process. In essay writing, they are born during the Grouping step and set in order during the Outlining step. Careful and thorough organization speeds paragraph writing and revision. With practice, writing paragraphs will become second nature for you.

Consider the following example:

EXAMPLE: A PARAGRAPH ABOUT PARAGRAPH WRITING

> *The **topic sentence** goes first and identifies what information is in the paragraph.* Then follows the information that supports the topic stated in the topic sentence. This information also supports the paper's thesis. The information can be in the form of facts, data, statistics, quotes from experts, examples, personal experience, case studies, or anything else that supports the topic. No matter what form the information comes in, the details must pertain to the paragraph's topic in a clear and understandable way.

Exercises

Write an essay on one of the following topics. Use the writing process to plan and prepare your paper. Complete each step as best you can as you move through the process.

1. Prepare and write an essay about an experience that changed you in some way: changed the way you think, the way you do something, the way you see a certain person, or the way you perceive life or the world. Explain the experience in enough detail so the reader can understand what happened and why it changed you.

2. Write an essay supporting the position that films and TV movies (or music videos) currently contain too much sex, perversity, and immorality. Support your thesis by using examples or scenes from actual films and movies (or music videos). Explain your examples clearly; don't assume that your readers have seen the same films, movies, or music videos you have.

3. Compare and contrast how you once felt about someone or some place or something as a child with how you feel about it now. Be clear about what is different between then and now. If possible, explain what changed your perspective.

CHAPTER 10

Writing Journals

| 1. Keeping a Journal | 2. Journal Possibilities |

1. KEEPING A JOURNAL

Keeping a journal is a good way to record your thoughts and observations. Journal writing allows you to connect to the world around you and to your experiences in life, in a personal and sometimes profound way. By their very nature, journals are as unique as the individuals writing them.

There are many approaches to journal writing, but most journal writers begin by keeping a daily log of their thoughts, feelings, and observations about the events of their life. Try to develop the habit of writing in your journal on a regular basis.

Sometimes professional people keep journals for recording the details of meetings, conferences, seminars, events, travels, and people they meet to help them in making presentations and for writing reports and proposals. Some keep them on computers. Professional writers and journalists also keep journals to help them recall the details of such things as events, people, travels, and personal experiences for writing articles, stories, and books.

NOTE: Some college instructors require "response journals." Usually this means writing your reaction to some assignment, such as a reading selection, film, show, or documentary. Often these are open-ended assignments, which means that you can respond in any manner you wish. (However, if serious analysis is required, see Chapter 11.)

2. JOURNAL POSSIBILITIES

For your journal, consider these possibilities:

- Record your reaction to daily events: personal experiences or world events. Include your thoughts, feelings, and insights.
- Describe certain people, events, places, incidents, or experiences that made an impression on you in some way. These could be personal (e.g., times with family or close friends), public (e.g., being at a sports event or on your college campus), or both.
- Write down your thoughts, feelings, and observations about things or people you have read about in books or the newspaper, or things you've seen in videos and films. Notice what kinds of things catch your eye or draw your attention. Consider the view of the world and the people in it that these media are presenting.
- Reflect on things from your past and speculate on how they have influenced you and helped make you who you are today. Consider how you have or have not changed.
- Write about your future: your hopes, dreams, goals, plans, and priorities. Don't just fantasize, but include things you want to accomplish and how you plan to accomplish them.
- Record your random thoughts, meditations, musings, dreams, ideas, or whatever. Let your mind or heart flow freely. Later you can look back and see if anything you wrote down is best left in the past or worth pursuing further.

For many, journal writing becomes a habit, even a lifelong pastime. Whether for a season or a lifetime, you may find journal writing a useful and enjoyable activity, a new way to connect you to life and the world around you.

EXAMPLE: SAMPLE JOURNAL ENTRY

> *Everything seems to have changed since September 11. I never used to be interested in the news or the world that much, but now I can't stop hearing about it. I listen to the news every day on the radio in my car and on TV when I'm home, and I read the newspaper—not just the sports and comics. I keep thinking about what happened and about how incredible and terrible it was. I can't get the images out of my mind. I keep seeing the planes exploding into the towers and then the towers collapsing in giant clouds of fire and smoke.*

Exercises

1. Begin keeping a daily journal that reflects mainly on your experience of attending college. Include not only observations, comments, and feelings about your college classes and instructors, but consider the entire college experience: people you meet, activities you attend (e.g., concerts, special lectures or performances, events and shows), dormitory living, working on campus, clubs or sports you participated in, and so on.
2. The next time you take a trip, keep a journal of your experiences, observations, thoughts, feelings, etc., about the places you go and the people you meet.
3. Begin keeping a reading journal in which you record your thoughts, musings, and opinions about what you have read in class or for pleasure.

CHAPTER 11

Responsive Writing: Analysis

1. College Classes	2.6 Thesis/Position
2. Analysis and Response	2.7 Outline
2.1 Read	2.8 Arrange
2.2 Reread	2.9 Write a Draft
2.3 Take Notes	2.10 Revision
2.4 Check	2.11 Proofread
2.5 Decide	2.12 Print

In the broadest sense, responsive writing can be any form of response to anything the writer wishes or is assigned to write about. Depending on the instructions given, the response could be a response to an assigned reading, a current event, a certain situation, a film or performance or TV show, an art exhibit, a sports contest, a person, a new law or policy, a personal experience, virtually anything. However, almost all responses require some kind of analysis.

1. COLLEGE CLASSES

In college classes, the subject you are to respond to is usually given as part of the assignment. In many college classes, written responses to assigned readings or current events or artistic performances are common requirements. The way in which you respond depends primarily on two things: the topic and the type of response requested.

Depending on the type of response requested, you may need to quote or paraphrase from the reading material, outline the structure of the writer's essay or story to explain why the writer succeeded or failed to make the point, or refer to your own personal experience and compare it to the writer's experience. Good responses often require different approaches, depending on what is requested. Evaluation, interpretation, synthesis, or comparison/contrast are all commonly requested types of analysis. However, your instructor will usually indicate what approach is required in the assignment instructions. Responsive writing follows many of the same steps as other types of writing, but it begins with analysis because you are responding to someone else's work or writing.

2. ANALYSIS AND RESPONSE

2.1 Read

Read the material carefully. Analysis requires good concentration, so find a quiet place. Try to see the overall picture and note how the writer handles the topic.

2.2 Reread

Read the material again. This time look for what is important and what stands out. Keep in mind what your analysis is supposed to show or accomplish. Note any significant information and specific details. Determine what the main points are and how the writer supports those points.

2.3 Take Notes

Mark important information you found in the reading material (mark photocopies if the text is not yours to write on) or take careful notes. Mark or record all major points and supporting details. Make an outline of the structure of the reading selection, if that helps you understand it better. Be sure to note the author's thesis or position on the topic.

2.4 Check

If your instructor has asked that certain kinds of information be included in your response, check your notes to make sure that information is there.

2.5 Decide

Decide what your response will be. Look carefully at your instructor's instructions. What kind of response is being requested? Will your response require a detailed synthesis of the material or will a discussion of the major point of the reading do the job? Will you need to quote from the material or will you merely reference the points you plan to discuss? Make your response fit the assignment given and address all aspects of what is requested.

2.6 Thesis/Position

Determine the major point you wish to make or the position you are going to take in response to the assigned reading material. Write down your thesis as a direct statement, preferably in one sentence. This will help guide your response.

2.7 Outline

Make a scratch outline of your response. In many cases, this outline will follow the pattern of the material you are responding to because it is easier and more logical to discuss the material in the order in which it was presented. For certain less formal forms of response, such as commentary or reflection, this is not necessarily true, but for most in-depth responses that require evaluation, interpretation, or synthesis, this outline works well and will be of significant help in organizing your response.

2.8 Arrange

Arrange your information to fit your outline. Decide where specific details or quotes are going to be placed in your analysis and response.

2.9 Write a Draft

Write a rough draft of your response. Writing analysis requires strong concentration, so work in a quiet place where you won't be disturbed. If possible, try to write your draft straight through. If not, try to write a section at a time without breaking your concentration. Write the draft through without worrying about such things as spelling, punctuation, and grammar. These should be handled after your revision.

2.10 Revision

Check your draft carefully against the material you are responding to and against the assignment you were given. Be sure that you've met the requirements and responded to all aspects the instructor asked for and in the manner requested. Then revise and rewrite as necessary to improve your response.

2.11 Proofread

After revision, remember to proofread for spelling, punctuation, grammatical errors, and so on.

2.12 Print

After checking your final draft carefully, print out a clean, clear copy.

Whatever type of response is required, it is generally best to name the subject of your response in the first sentence of the introduction (for example, title and author if responding to a reading) and mention your thesis or main idea somewhere in the introductory paragraph. (See Figure 11.1.)

Instructors usually assign responsive writing to challenge your skills of analysis. They want to know what you think about something. Just tell them, as clearly as you can.

Figure 11.1 Sample Response: Analysis

A Brief Analysis of the *Declaration of Independence*

by Sandy Wilson

The *Declaration of Independence,* written by Thomas Jefferson, is in the form of a classic argument. In the first paragraphs, Jefferson presents the issue and gives necessary background information to establish the claim that the "United States" of America have the right to be free of British rule. The basis of his premise is, "We hold these truths to be self-evident, that all men are created equal, that they are endowed by their Creator with certain inalienable rights, that among these are life, liberty and the pursuit of happiness."

Jefferson goes on to say that securing these rights is the purpose of government, and any government that is destructive of these ends should be altered or abolished and a new government established in its place. He acknowledges, however, that such drastic measures should not be taken or instituted lightly, but only when there is evidence of "a long train of abuses and usurpations." Jefferson then states that the king of Great Britain is guilty of such tyranny.

The greater part of the body of the *Declaration of Independence* is a detailed list of twenty-eight grievances the colonists had against King George III and the British government. These are offered as proof of Jefferson's claim that serious and repeated violations have occurred and that, therefore, the colonists have the right to separate themselves from British rule and form a new government. These grievances are addressed to the other countries of the world for their consideration (and, hopefully, approval).

The twenty-eight grievances fall into two general categories: governmental abuses and human rights' violations. They include things such as refusal to pass necessary laws for governing the people, dissolving representative bodies, obstructing the administration of justice, keeping standing armies among the people in peace time, cutting off trade with the rest of the world, taxation without representation, depriving people of trial by jury, and abolishing laws. In addition, the king was sending armies of foreign mercenaries against the colonists to subdue them.

Jefferson then assures his world audience that repeated attempts to redress these grievances have been made but all were refused. He continues to explain that the colonists have warned their British brethren of how the legislature has attempted to "extend an unwarrantable jurisdiction" over them, but they too have ignored the colonists.

In the concluding paragraph, Jefferson declares and forcefully reinforces his claim that the "United Colonies" are and have the right to be free states, independent of the British Crown and government, free to establish their own government as they see fit. To emphasize the resolve of the supporters of the *Declaration of Independence,* Jefferson states, ". . . we mutually pledge to each other our lives, our fortunes, and our sacred honor."

Exercises

Write a response for one of the following. Use analysis and the writing process to plan and prepare your paper. Complete each step as best you can as you move through the process.

1. Respond to an essay or reading selection in your English textbook. Analyze the author's main point and key support points. Then agree or disagree with the author and write a brief paper clarifying your position.

2. Write an in-depth analysis of a short story. Determine the main point the author is making in the story. Analyze other related literary elements, such as plot, characterization, setting, theme, language, and point of view, and explain how these elements contribute to the story.

3. Select an article on a controversial issue from a newspaper or a weekly news magazine, such as *Time* or *US News & World Report*. Analyze the article to determine its main point as well as the key support points and details. Write your analysis in essay form.

4. (Alternate) Exchange essays with another student. Analyze the paper for content, logic, and coherence. Write comments on the paper's strengths and weaknesses. If appropriate, tactfully offer suggestions for improving the paper (refer to Chapter 5).

CHAPTER 12

Writing Laboratory or Field Reports

1. Introduction (or Purpose)	4. Results (Findings or Data)
2. Materials	5. Discussion/Conclusions
3. Methods (or Procedures)	

Scientific reports follow a basic structure. Laboratory (lab) and field reports are used in the natural and physical sciences and for social science research projects to describe experiments, to record observations, and to draw conclusions based on your findings. Although scientific reports aren't structured like essays, nor do they read like them, they share some elements of essay writing. Good scientific reports rely on thorough description and reporting of facts. Clarity is very important. The sections are usually titled or labeled (as discussed below). The structure of lab or field reports allows for some variation, but the basic sections remain the same (see Figure 12.1, p. 40). Remember, this is just a guideline; be sure to follow the format recommended by your instructor.

1. INTRODUCTION (OR PURPOSE)

Begin by stating the purpose or the objective of the experiment or field study. Also explain the scope (extent or range) of the experiment or field study and provide any background information necessary for understanding the purpose, objective, or scope of the experiment. Remember to present your hypothesis, your expectation of the results of the experiment. If you are doing a field report, you may wish to include a map and description of the location of your field area.

If you are doing a field study, it may be important to note any weather conditions on the day(s) and time(s) you are on location (e.g., temperature, humidity, wind, rain), as well as any other observations that are pertinent to your experiment or study. It's a good idea to keep a log book (notebook) for recording field study information and observations.

2. MATERIALS

Describe all equipment and apparatus used in the experiment, one by one. If the list is not extensive, it is sometimes combined with the Methods (or Procedures) section.

3. METHODS (OR PROCEDURES)

Describe how the experiment or field study was conducted, including how the equipment and apparatus were used. Explain how the experiment was set up or how the field study was done, from beginning to end, like telling a story or giving an account. Mention if you had a control set or if you ran multiple trials of your experiment. Your description should be clear enough that someone else could duplicate the experiment or field study after reading this section.

4. RESULTS (FINDINGS OR DATA)

Summarize the results or findings of the experiment or field study. Include only significant information pertaining to what you found (or didn't find). Use charts, graphs, illustrations, photos, or other means to help your readers follow and understand what happened and precisely what the results were. Be sure to clearly label graphs, charts, or illustrations and show measurements and units used in the experiment.

5. DISCUSSION/CONCLUSIONS

Interpret and evaluate the results. Explain as best you can what the results mean and why they support (or don't support) the hypothesis. If they don't support the hypothesis, speculate or suggest a reason why. Tell what conclusions or implications can be drawn from the results of the experiment or field study. Use evidence from the experiment or field study to support your discussion and your conclusions. You may also include recommendations for future studies or suggest ways you might modify the experiment to optimize the results. (NOTE: Some instructors prefer that Discussion and Conclusions be separate sections. Follow your instructor's preference.)

Formal scientific reports also require a title page and an abstract (see Chapters 14 and 15) at the beginning. Typically, a list of references appears at the end of the report. This list includes sources used in the literature survey conducted before the experiment or field study began and/or any sources cited in the report itself. Be sure to follow the accepted documentation format; for example, natural sciences use the Council of Biology Editors (CBE) documentation style.

Figure 12.1 Sample Lab Report

Initial Report on Barn Owl Diet in Audubon County Wildlife Study

Stan Wells and Melissa Vang
Biology 115
Dr. Kim Longbow
October 27, 2002

Introduction: This is the initial report on the diet of barn owls (*Tyto alba*) in Audubon County. It is part of a broader, ten-year long wildlife study sponsored by the county Agricultural Commission and conducted by the City College biology department. The purpose of this study is to determine the preferred food of barn owls and to understand the implications in the larger ecological study of the county.

Audubon County is 67 percent farmland and woodland, and rodents are a significant problem for farmers and crops. Initial studies indicate that barn owls, which are nocturnal hunters, are important rodent predators. The study involved studying pellets (casts) of twenty barn owls throughout the county over a six-month period.

Methods and Materials: Obtaining and examining barn owl pellets (casts) involved a two-step process. First, twenty (20) known barn owl nests (from a previous survey) across Audubon County were visited every weekend for six months and samples of owl pellets were collected. Samples were collected in plastic baggies using latex gloves. Baggies were labeled by site name and location (see map in Appendix A).

Second, in the laboratory, pellet samples were individually examined and their contents recorded. Samples were taken apart using needle probes and small forceps. Skulls and bones found in the samples were separated and catalogued by visually comparing them (skulls, mainly) with those in the City College skeletal collection and with illustrations in H. R. Hansen's *Rodent Anatomy and Physiology* (1998). After identification, they were categorized as mice, shrews, voles, other rodent, non-rodent, or unidentified, and then counted. Twenty-five (25) field reports were completed.

Results: In all, 1,575 samples were examined and catalogued. The barn owls in the study ate mostly mice (944); the two species preferred being the common field mouse and the deer mouse, comprising 60 percent of their diet. Next most consumed were common shrews (236) and meadow voles (158), 15 percent and 10 percent, respectively. Other

(continued)

rodents (63) accounted for 4 percent. Non-rodent (143), mostly reptiles, comprised 9 percent. Just 2 percent (31) were not able to be identified (see Figure 1).

Figure 1   Barn Owl Diet: Audubon County Wildlife Study, 2002

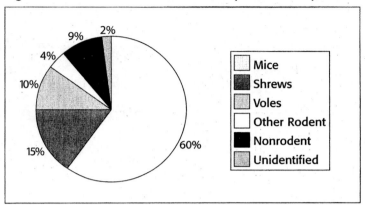

Conclusions: Barn owls are obviously significant predators, especially of rodents, although they will occasionally take other small mammals and reptiles. They prefer mice, shrews, and voles. It is clear that they are useful to farmers in helping control rodent populations and protecting crops.

Reference:

Hansen H R. Rodent anatomy and physiology. Oxford: Oxford Univ Pr; 1998. 611p.

Exercises

Note: *You should never use a laboratory or the laboratory equipment without your instructor's permission and supervision.*

Although your instructors will assign you laboratory or field exercises to report on, you can collect your own observations and specimens on outings or field trips you take. Reports are built from laboratory and field notes.

1. Take a field hike and collect observations in a field notebook about the plants and animals you see. Be sure to include a description of the habitat areas where you observed the plants and animals in your survey.
2. Pick a particular habitat that animals frequent, such as a stream, pond, watering hole, or trail, and find a vantage point from which to observe from a distance. Keep a log of the animals that come and go throughout the hours of an entire day. Include observations about their behavior and habits.
3. Take a field trip to collect specimens of something you are interested in studying or identifying, such as plants, insects, or rock samples. Record where each specimen came from. If removing samples is not advisable or not allowed, sketch pictures of specimens into your field notebook or take color photographs of them. Then use a published field guide to identify your collection.

CHAPTER 13

Writing a Case Study and Analysis

1. Doing Case Analysis	2. Writing Case Analysis
1.1 Read	2.1 Gather Information
1.2 Study	2.2 Position/Solution
1.3 Research	2.3 Summarize
1.4 Analyze	2.4 Possible Solutions
1.5 Solutions	2.5 Best Solution
1.6 Decide	2.6 Implementation

Case studies are often used in social science and business courses to teach critical thinking skills used to evaluate situations and solve problems. The situation given usually presents a set of circumstances or behaviors and relates the resulting problems. The challenge is to analyze the situation, determine the key issues and the people involved, then present a reasonable and workable solution. (See Figure 13.1.)

Careful analysis is the key to good case study. Depending on the situation given, there may be more than one viable solution to a problem. Providing a clear and logical analysis and solution is the goal. Like other types of writing, case analysis follows a basic pattern. (See Figure 13.2, p. 44.)

1. DOING CASE ANALYSIS

1.1 Read

Read the entire case through, slowly. Familiarize yourself with the situation presented and the information given.

1.2 Study

Carefully reread the case and determine the key points and people involved. Pick out the important details and issues that relate to the major problems. Mark them or write them down.

1.3 Research

If your case is complicated, you may need to search out additional information that is not presented in the case profile. This usually involves research on the key pieces of information you identified in your case study. (See Chapter 19.)

1.4 Analyze

Determine why the problems exist and what or who causes them. Analyze how the various aspects of the situation are related to each other and to the resulting problems. Also determine which people are key to the situation and how they relate to others and the problems encountered. It may help to take careful notes.

1.5 Solutions

Consider possible solutions to the situation and problems presented. Use what you know and what you've learned to draft plans and to generate reasonable solutions.

1.6 Decide

Weigh the strengths and weaknesses of the possible solutions to the problem(s). Determine the best overall solution. Be sure that it addresses the critical aspects of the situation and that it is reasonable and workable.

Make notes on why you arrived at your decision and what your thought process was, and include any support information from your analysis and research.

2. WRITING CASE ANALYSIS

Writing case analysis requires careful attention to detail and a clear and logical presentation. Your goal is to present a brief but thorough explanation of the case, including a summary of the situation and the key points and people involved. Intersperse the explanation with your analysis, a discussion of the possible solutions, your choice of the best solution (supported by facts and logic), and your advice on implementing the solution. The pattern that follows explains the process and provides a commonly used structure for a case analysis report.

2.1 Gather Information

As with any piece of writing, when moving from thinking and analysis to writing, begin by gathering the information you need to support your position, in this case, your solution.

2.2 Position/Solution

Your solution should be stated as a thesis, naming the topic and your position, in the first or second paragraph of the paper. Be clear and direct.

2.3 Summarize

Provide enough background information so that your reader will understand the context of your analysis. Don't just repeat the case; summarize the situation and the key information regarding the issues and people involved. Relate only the details that are essential to an understanding of the situation and your analysis of it. If the case is complex or involved, you may want to break it down into sections; for example, state a point of the case, then follow with the analysis.

2.4 Possible Solutions

It is not usually required that you discuss in great detail all the possible solutions you considered, but you should explain the solutions that you considered and tell why you rejected them. Generally, solutions are rejected because of their weaknesses and shortcomings.

Figure 13.1 Sample Case Study

Sam liked being a college student, but as midterms approached he was becoming concerned. This had been a big year for him so far. He was enrolled full time at City College, he worked 30 to 35 hours per week at his favorite computer store, and he had finally been able to move from his parents' home to a place with his two best friends, Nick and Jamie. His parents had harassed him about spending all his money on video games, computer accessories, and movies when he'd lived at home. Now it took most of his money just to survive, but he valued his freedom. He and Nick and Jamie could do whatever they wanted when they wanted, if they weren't in class or at work. Going to college and working and living on their own made life hectic, but they liked it. However, there just wasn't enough time for everything between going to college full time and working so many hours. For Sam, finding time to study was often a real problem because Nick and Jamie also liked to party. Life was fun, but Sam found he was increasingly tired and his grades were dropping dramatically. He was in danger of failing two courses. He knew he had to do something but he wasn't sure what.

Figure 13.2 Sample Case Analysis

Summary

Sam's situation is not uncommon among college students. He is fully engaged in his life, but is beginning to realize that he may have taken on more than he can handle at this time. Living away from home for the first time and trying to go to college full time while working 30 to 35 hours per week would be daunting for most adults, and most wouldn't attempt it. As Sam has come to realize, there are only so many hours in a day, and having roommates who like to party does not help the situation. Sam seems to realize that he doesn't have or allow enough time for studying, but he doesn't know what to change to make more time to study. Sam needs to take an aggressive three-pronged approach to work less, party less, and study more.

Possible Solutions

One possible solution to Sam's dilemma is to give up his apartment and his roommates and move back home. Assuming his parents' home offers a less hectic, more stable environment, he would be likely to find more study time there. The downside is that he'd have to give up his freedom and learning how to be on his own. His grades would probably improve, but he would be back under his parents' scrutiny.

Another possible solution would be to quit working and take on college as a full-time responsibility, then work on getting good grades and graduating as soon as possible. Many students do this, but most who do it live away from home, usually in another town. The main drawback is that without his job, Sam probably can't afford to live away from home and would have to move back, creating essentially the same situation as the first possibility, but he also wouldn't have any spending money.

A third possibility that would appeal to most college students would be to buckle down, quit partying with his roommates, and become disciplined. Instead of partying, Sam could pack his books and head to the library whenever a party broke out. This might allow him, in theory, to keep his apartment and his job, and to salvage his grades. However, this is not realistic. It doesn't address the main problem: Sam has taken on too much. Even if he could summon the discipline, he would still be going to college fulltime and working 30 to 35 hours per week. Very few could handle this pace of life. He would still have to have some relaxation and down time; we all do. This does not mean that limits shouldn't be established on having parties, but time to relax or recreate is necessary to keep us balanced and healthy. This would be only a partial solution.

Solution

Sam's best solution would be a three-pronged approach. Going to college full time and working 30 to 35 hours per week is not for most people. Assuming Sam doesn't want to return home, he needs to immediately cut back on work hours or class hours, or both. Studies indicate that most students cannot go to college full time and work more than 10-15 hours per week, depending on how demanding their class work is. Sam needs to determine how many hours a week he needs to work to stay in the apartment. If that is more than 15, and it probably is, then he should cut back on his course load. Realistically, college courses require 2 to 3 hours outside of class for every hour spent in class each week. Sam should consider working part time and going to college part time. He might start by dropping one or both of the classes he is failing. Sam should also cut back on the partying. He and his roommates need to come to an agreement on limiting their parties to, say, one weekend per month. This may seem drastic, but if one or more of them flunk out, they will likely lose their apartment. They also need to get serious about making time to study and get good grades. Exercising a reasoned and disciplined approach is the best chance Sam and his roommates have for maintaining their freedom while still getting an education.

2.5 Best Solution

Discuss in detail the solution you think is best. Explain why you think it is best by supporting its positive points with facts and logic taken from your analysis.

2.6 Implementation

You might also suggest how you think your solution could be implemented. (Out of necessity, this may flow from the discussion of your solution.) Be specific about your advice on how to change the situation or personnel. If you think new methods or policies are needed, say so, and explain what they should say and do. If you think it helpful, include a timetable to implement your solution. Be clear on what should happen and when.

Write your case analysis and solution in standard essay or report style. It is often helpful to use subtitles to show the different sections of your analysis. Try to be as clear and direct as possible in explaining your perspective on the case and on your solution.

Exercises

1. Consider the following case and write an analysis.

    > Barb Stevens is the floor manager for Home Hardware in Bay Town. Home Hardware is a fairly large store with ten departments. Each department has a manager with 20 to 30 years of experience in their trade (paint, gardening, lumber, electrical, etc.). However, every summer season Barb runs short of experienced department managers when vacation time arrives. Each manager is allowed 3 to 4 weeks of vacation per year. When July arrives, four or five department managers might be gone at any one time. This creates problems because summer is also a very busy season with homeowners and others working on projects around the house and yard. Customers rely on the managers for expert advice. The salespeople in each department do their best to cover when the managers aren't there, but most are hourly workers without the years of experience the managers have.
    >
    > Managers work five eight-hour days or four ten-hour days, depending on the time of year. Weekends are mandatory in busy months. Barb hires vacation replacements, but few have the seasoned experience of the full-time managers. Those that have experience lack knowledge of the Home Hardware store layout and other aspects. Also, good substitutes are hard to find because few people with the expertise and experience required are available for just three or four weeks out of the year, especially in the summer. Nor are many people willing to work for temporary wages and no benefits (benefit packages are not available for temporary employees). However, Barb's boss is insistent that she find a solution before next summer.

2. Consider a situation you know about or have encountered at work or school. Write up the case, presenting the facts to the best of your knowledge. Then, after carefully examining the facts, write an analysis of the situation and the people involved and offer a solution.
3. Examine a case or article published in a professional journal. Write your own analysis and offer a solution to the situation.

CHAPTER 14

Writing Abstracts and Executive Summaries

1. Types of Abstracts and Executive Summary
2. Preparation
   2.1 Study Document or Article
   2.2 Get an Overview
   2.3 Mark Key Information
   2.4 Identify Topic, Purpose, Methods, etc.
3. Writing a Descriptive Abstract
   3.1 Identify Topic and Purpose
   3.2 Identify Methods
   3.3 Tell Contents of Report
   3.4 List Key Words
   3.5 Check Summary against Document

4. Writing an Informative Abstract or Executive Summary
   4.1 Identify Topic and Purpose
   4.2 Identify Methods
   4.3 Explain Results/Findings
   4.4 Tell Conclusions and Recommendations
   4.5 Tell Contents of Report
   4.6 List Key Words
   4.7 Check Summary against Document

Summarizing the key points of a report or document allows readers to grasp essential information quickly. Abstracts and executive summaries are synopses or concise overviews of reports, proposals, procedures, and research articles. They are a condensed version of the document, paraphrased only, without quoting from the document. Think of them as summary information, not commentary.

Abstracts and executive summaries include the key points of the document's introduction, thesis or hypothesis, the results or findings, and the conclusions and recommendations. The summary information must be brief, but also complete and accurate.

Abstracts and executive summaries appear on a separate page after the title page and are written in block paragraph format, using complete sentences, double-spacing, and no paragraph indentations. The word(s) "Abstract" or "Executive Summary" should be centered at the top of the page.

1. TYPES OF ABSTRACTS AND EXECUTIVE SUMMARY

Two types of abstracts are used. **Descriptive abstracts** are very brief, two to four sentences in one short paragraph, and they simply tell the content of the document for which they are written, with no key information given.

Informative abstracts may run up to 200 to 300 words (APA style, about 100 words, 960 characters), and they tell the key information contained in the document. Abstracts are usually written for readers with technical or other special expertise.

Executive summaries also tell all the key information, but they may run one to three pages (but not over 10 percent of the document's total length) and are usually written for management-level executives and decision makers.

Writing abstracts and executive summaries is a two-step process.

2. PREPARATION

2.1 Study Document or Article

If the abstract or executive summary is for your own report or document, finish writing the report or document before trying to summarize it. On the other hand, if you are writing an abstract or executive summary of someone else's work, read and study the document carefully.

2.2 Get an Overview

Get a clear overview of the document and what is being reported.

2.3 Mark Key Information

Go through the document again, marking key information, subheadings, and so on, then write a scratch outline of the sections and information.

2.4 Identify Topic, Purpose, Method, etc.

Determine and list the topic, purpose, scope, methods, results, conclusions, and recommendations reported in the document.

Following are examples of a Descriptive Abstract (Figure 14.1), an Informative Abstract (Figure 14.2, p. 48), and an Executive Summary (Figure 14.3, p. 49), all based on the same report in Chapter 12.

3. WRITING A DESCRIPTIVE ABSTRACT

3.1 Identify Topic and Purpose

Identify the topic or project being reported on in the document.

3.2 Identify Methods

Describe the work done and the method(s) used. Do not include results, conclusions, or recommendations.

3.3 Tell Contents of Report

Describe the document's major contents.

3.4 List Key Words

List three to eight key words that would help someone find the document's information in a database or index.

Figure 14.1 Sample Descriptive Abstract

Abstract

This report is the first on the diet of barn owls (*Tyto alba*) in Audubon County, part of a broader, ten-year wildlife, ecological study. Barn owl pellets (casts) were collected and studied over a six-month period. Rodent skulls and bones in the pellets were separated, identified, and catalogued. Initial findings and conclusions are included.

Key words: barn owl, *Tyto alba,* Audubon County wildlife study, owl pellets, rodent skulls

3.5 Check Summary against Document

Check your abstract against the document for accuracy and clarity.
   (NOTE: See the lab report in Chapter 12 for the source of these abstracts.)

4. WRITING AN INFORMATIVE ABSTRACT OR EXECUTIVE SUMMARY

4.1 Identify Topic and Purpose

Identify the topic or project being reported on and indicate the purpose of the project.

4.2 Identify Methods

Give key details of the methods or procedures used.

4.3 Explain Results/Findings

Give a brief explanation or analysis of the results or findings.

4.4 Tell Conclusions and Recommendations

Tell what conclusions and recommendations were made and any implications or applications that were mentioned.

4.5 Tell Contents of Report

Tell the contents of the report that follows.

4.6 List Key Words

List three to eight key words that would help someone find the document's information in a database or index. (Executive summaries don't always list key words.)

Figure 14.2 Sample Informative Abstract

Abstract

The initial study on the diet of barn owls (*Tyto alba*) in Audubon County is presented as part of a broader, ten-year wildlife, ecological study. The purpose of the study is to determine the preferred food of barn owls and the implications in the larger study and to Audubon County agriculture. Over a six-month period, pellets (casts) from 20 barn owls in locations throughout Audubon County were collected and examined. Rodent skulls and bones were separated using needle probes and small forceps, then identified and catalogued. Some 1,575 samples were examined. Initial results indicate that the barn owls' diet consists of mice (60%), shrews (15%), voles (10%), other rodents (4%), nonrodent (9%), and unidentified (2%). Obviously, barn owls are significant predators, especially of rodents, preferring mice, shrews, and voles. Clearly they help to control rodent populations and protect crops. Barn owls, and their impact as predators, appear to make them a key species among Audubon County wildlife.
Key words: barn owl, *Tyto alba*, Audubon County wildlife study, owl pellets, rodent skulls

4.7 Check Summary against Document

Check your abstract or executive summary against the document for accuracy and clarity.

Figure 14.3 Sample Executive Summary

> ### Executive Summary
> ### Initial Study of the Diet of Barn Owls
> ### for the Audubon County Agricultural Commission
> ### October 27, 2002
>
> The initial study on the diet of barn owls (*Tyto alba*) in Audubon County has been completed as part of a broader, ten-year wildlife, ecological study. The purpose of the study is to determine the preferred food of barn owls and the implications in the larger ecological study and any benefit to Audubon County agriculture. Over a six-month period, 20 barn owls sites in locations throughout Audubon County were routinely examined. Rodent skulls and bones were collected, then identified and catalogued. Some 1,575 samples were examined and recorded in 25 separate field reports.
>
> Initial results indicate that the barn owls' diet consists of mice (60%), shrews (15%), voles (10%), other rodents (4%), non-rodent (9%), and unidentified (2%). Obviously, barn owls are significant predators, especially of rodents, preferring mice, shrews, and voles. Clearly they help to control rodent populations and protect agricultural crops. Barn owls, and their impact as predators, appear to make them a key species among Audubon County wildlife. Further study will give a more complete picture of how barn owls are integral to the ecological balance in Audubon County and how they benefit agricultural productivity.

Remember to keep abstracts and summaries brief and direct while clearly stating the essential points of the report or document.

Exercises

1. Select an article or report from a professional journal in your field of study and write a descriptive abstract. Include a copy of the article or report if you must turn in your abstract.
2. Select an article or report from a professional journal in your field of study and write an informative abstract. Include a copy of the article or report if you must turn in your abstract.
3. Select a business or government report and write an executive summary. Include a copy of the article or report if you must turn in your executive summary.

Part III:
BASIC DOCUMENT DESIGN AND FORMAT

Standardized formats have been developed for most documents, whether college papers or professional work. The **format** is how the document is laid out on the page, and it affects the way a document reads and how readers react to the document. College teachers and other professionals expect that you will follow standard document formats.

CHAPTER 15
College Paper Format

1. Formatting Guidelines
   1.1 Paper and Binding   1.4 Pagination
   1.2 Font and Ink   1.5 Title Page or Identification Block
   1.3 Margins and Spacing   1.6 A Note on Electronic Submissions

1. FORMATTING GUIDELINES

Writing papers or essays is one of the most common assignments given in college classes. The experience of writing papers not only allows instructors to evaluate your learning and understanding of various topics, it also teaches valuable skills in written communication. College paper writing is the basis for the type of writing you will do later in professional life. Learning college paper format will also make your college life easier and improve your grades.

The following are standard, but you should follow your teacher's instructions.

1.1 Paper and Binding

Use standard 8 1/2 by 11 inch white bond paper, 20-pound weight. Avoid using erasable papers because ink tends to smear on these kinds of papers. Separate all pages and clip them together with a staple or paper clip in the upper left hand corner. Use a presentation folder if something more formal is required.

1.2 Font and Ink

Use a common, readable serif-style typeface for the text, such as Times New Roman or Courier, 10 to 12 point in size. Use lower and upper case lettering in the text. Do not use all capitals. Avoid fancy or script style typefaces because they quickly become difficult to read after a page or so. You might want to use a sans serif typeface, such as Arial or Helvetica, for headings and subheadings to help set them off and make them stand out. Headings can also be put in **boldface** and be in a larger size type, such as 14 point, but don't use large type size for the text in an attempt to stretch the length of your paper. Experienced college teachers can quickly spot the larger type. Use black ink only for the text and headings, unless you are told otherwise. However, color may be used for illustrations, graphs, charts, and so on.

1.3 Margins and Spacing

Use 1 to 1 1/2 inch margins on all sides, double space all text, use left margin justification (not full), and indent the first line of each paragraph 1/2 inch (usually one tab). Leave only one space after punctuation marks (commas, periods, colons, semicolons, questions marks, exclamation points).

1.4 Pagination

Put your last name and the page number in Arabic numerals (i.e., 1, 2, 3, 4) in the upper left or right hand corner, whichever your instructor requires, 1/2 inch from the top of the page.

1.5 Title Page or Identification Block

Formal papers generally require a **title page** or **cover sheet**. About one-third of the way down the page, center and type the title of your paper using upper and lowercase letters. Capitalize the first letter of the first word, last word, and all other major words in the title. Do not use italics, underlining, quotation marks, boldface, or all capital letters. Double-space and type "by." Double-space again and type your name.

About half way down the page, type the name and number of the course the paper was written for, as well as the class section number (if required). Double-space and type your instructor's name, preceded by "Dr." or "Professor," if requested by your instructor. Double-space again and type in the due date of the paper (not the date you did the paper, but date it is due). (See Example 15.1, p. 52.)

Less formal or short papers often require only an **identification block** in the upper left hand corner of the first page, double-spaced. Along the left margin, first type your name, then the instructor's name, again using "Dr." or "Professor," if requested. Follow this information with the course name and number, and then the due date. Double-space again before centering your title. (See Example 15.2, p. 53.)

1.6 A Note on Electronic Submissions

If you are allowed to or requested to submit your paper electronically, beware that if you paste it into the screen it will lose most of its formatting, especially spacing and fonts, special characters, and so on. If submitting electronically, send your paper as an attachment to preserve your formatting. Check ahead of time to make sure you are using compatible word processing software that your instructor can download and read. NOTE: Be extra careful not to send a virus with your attachment. You may want to send a copy of your submission to yourself so you can check it over for formatting problems before sending it to your instructor.

Example 15.1 Sample College Paper Title Page or Cover Sheet

Title starts 1/3 page from top

The Panay Incident

by
Ryan Rooks

Title

Your Name

Course ID block starts about halfway from top

World History 201

Professor S. Calhoun

October 18, 2002

Course Name and Number

Professor's Name

Due Date

Example 15.2 Sample College Paper Title Page with Identification Block

Your Name

Professor's Name
Course Name and Number
Due Date

Ryan Rooks   Rooks 1

Professor S. Calhoun

World History 201

October 18, 2002

Your Last Name and the Page Number

Title

The Panay Incident

On the afternoon of December 12, 1937, a large U.S. military patrol boat drifted down the Yangtze River, leading a flotilla of other boats. The sky was calm and fairly clear. Sniper fire emanated from the bushes on the shoreline but was not really a threat. The buzz of Japanese planes reverberated through the mess hall below decks where the majority of the crew sat. The whistle of the tail fins on the aerial bombs gave little alert before the first wave thundered into the forward deck. For several long moments, chaos reigned. The ensuing battle became one of the most infamous incidents in U.S. and Japanese history.

In the summer of 1937, Japan was definitely expanding. Its forces swept southward and westward into eastern China and Manchuria. China declared war on Japan in June. At the time, Japan clearly had the better military forces, but they were divided. Japan's army was mainly preoccupied with fighting Russia, and its navy was also spread thin. Many other countries, including the United States, were acting as neutral third parties. They were engaged in various humanitarian efforts, including helping to remove civilians from the war zone.

Five U.S. and British ships were sent as river gunboats. One of these, the USS Panay commanded by Commander J. J. Hughes, was used as a gunship along the Yangtze River. The Panay had actually been built ten years earlier as a patrol boat during the Chinese civil war period. It was a large ship at over 190 feet long and 450-ton displacement. It had a crew compliment of 65.

CHAPTER 16
Business Letter Format

1. Standard Letter Parts	**2. Optional Letter Parts**
1.1 Letterhead or Return Address	2.1 Initials
1.2 Date	2.2 Enclosure
1.3 Inside Address	2.3 Copy
1.4 Reference or Subject Line	
1.5 Salutation or Greeting	
1.6 Body	
1.7 Complimentary Close	
1.8 Signature Space	
1.9 Signature Name	
1.10 Title or Position	

Business letters are for correspondence addressed to parties outside the company or agency (although sometimes they are sent between divisions within a large company or corporation). Use letterhead stationery or 8 1/2 by 11 inch white bond, 20-pound weight paper. Use 1 to 1 1/2 inch margins. Single-space within letter parts and double-space between each part (except the signature space). Use block or semi-block page format and center the letter vertically on the page.

Block format aligns all parts of the letter against the left margin (see Example 16.1, p. 56). Semi-block format also uses left margin alignment, but aligns the return address, date, and signature block to the right of the vertical center line of the page (see Example 16.2, p. 57). Margins can be set at left or full justification.

1. STANDARD LETTER PARTS

1.1 Letterhead or Return Address

Use letterhead stationery, if available. If not, type your **return address**, single-spaced, on two lines, starting with your street address, followed by city, state, and ZIP code. Do **not** include your name in the return address.

1.2 Date

Use month, day, year (or day, month, year) and spell out the month (e.g. June 30, 2002).

1.3 Inside Address

At the left margin, type the name and location of the person to receive the letter. Use Mr., Ms., Dr., or whatever title is appropriate, and the name of a specific person, including their title or position (i.e., CEO, Manager). If the addressee has a long title, use a separate line for it. (Do not use "To Whom It May Concern" or the like.) If you don't know the person's name, check the company's Web site or call the company and ask. (It's okay to ask.) Follow this with the company or agency name, street address, city, state, and ZIP code.

1.4 Reference or Subject Line

This is optional but is becoming standard. Indicate or refer to the subject of your letter. Also, reference any claim, account, or order numbers.

1.5 Salutation or Greeting

Type "Dear Mr. (or Ms. or Dr.)" and the last name of the person to whom the letter is addressed. Do not use first names in formal correspondence. If you cannot tell from the name if the addressee is male or female, then standard practice is to call the company switchboard and ask. Don't guess. Follow the salutation with a **colon** (:).

1.6 Body

This is the text of your message. Single space within paragraphs and double space between them. Indenting first lines of paragraphs is optional, but follow the same style for every paragraph, whether you indent or not.

1.7 Complimentary Close

Use "Sincerely," or "Sincerely yours," or the less formal, "Regards."

1.8 Signature Space

Leave four lines of space for signing your name. Write it in ink.

1.9 Signature Name

Type your name under where your signature will go. It will clearly identify you (many of us have signatures that are hard to read). Women may indicate Mrs., Miss, or Ms. before their name (in parentheses) if they wish, but this is not required.

1.10 Title or Position

Type your title or position name under your name if you are representing your company or agency in this correspondence.

2. OPTIONAL LETTER PARTS

Optional letter parts provide additional information. Double-space between all optional letter parts. Only the most common are described here.

2.1 Initials

Initials indicate that someone other than the letter writer actually typed the letter. The writer's initials (use *all* initials with no periods) appear in capital letters, separated by a colon (:) or a slash (/) from the typist's initials, which appear in lower case (e.g., RMS/tbp).

2.2 Enclosure (Enc: or Encl:)

This indicates that something is enclosed with the letter and usually names what it is (e.g., Encl: Resume *or* Enc: Parts Invoice).

2.3 Copy (cc: or c:)

Name any one that received a copy of the letter, by name or title (c: Marketing Director).

Example 16.1 Sample Business Letter—Block Flush Left Format on Letterhead

Letterhead Block

City College of California
Humanities Division
678 N. Sierra Rd
Foothill, CA 95188
(493) 357-1126

Date

14 May 2002

Inside Address

Gabriel Martinez, Admissions Officer
Pacific Bay University
1135 Grand Ave
Pacific Bay, CA 92775

Reference Line

Re: Recommendation for Rachel V. Rodriquez

Salutation

Dear Mr. Martinez:

Body

It is my pleasure to recommend Rachel V. Rodriquez for admission to Pacific Bay University. I became acquainted with Rachel when she enrolled in my English 3 course last spring.

English 3 is the required critical thinking course and most of our students find the class quite challenging. The course culminates in a formal research paper and oral presentation. Many students find the course work daunting, but Rachel excelled in all aspects. Her research paper on the presidential election and the Electoral College was very well done.

I find Rachel an excellent and hardworking student. She is a good writer and learns quickly. She has indicated that she plans to major in English or Communications, with an eye toward teaching. I am confident that she will do well. I highly recommend her and I encourage you to accept her application.

Complimentary Close

Sincerely,

Signature Space

Terry Vosberg

Name, Title Department Name

Terry Vosberg, Ph.D.
Composition Department

Example 16.2 Sample Business Letter—Semi-Block Format

Return Address	1515 Courtney Ave #303 College Place, CA 97998
Date	20 May 2002
Inside Address	Gabriel Martinez, Admissions Officer Pacific Bay University 1135 Grand Ave Pacific Bay, CA 92775
Salutation	Dear Mr. Martinez:
Body	Please accept my application for admission to Pacific Bay University for the fall term 2002. Included is my completed application form. I have made arrangements to have my transcripts from City College, my SAT scores, and my three letters of recommendation forwarded to your office by June 30, 2002.
	I understand that if my grades and general education units are acceptable, I will be admitted as a transfer student in good standing for this fall term. After the semester just finished, I have a 2.87 GPA and 60 semester units. If accepted, I will declare as a Liberal Arts major with the intent of becoming an elementary school teacher.
	You may reach me at the address above until June 15. After that date, I will be residing at 394 Willow Rd, Modesto, CA 95350, my "permanent address."
	Thank you for your time and consideration.
Complimentary Close	Sincerely,
Signature Space	*Rachel V. Rodriquez*
Name	Rachel V. Rodriquez
Enclosure	Encl: application

CHAPTER 17

Memorandum Format

---

1. Memo Headings	**2. Body**
1.1 DATE	**3. Optional Memo Parts**
1.2 TO	3.1 Reference Initials
1.3 FROM	3.2 Attachment Notice
1.4 SUBJECT	

Generally, memoranda (memos) are used within a company or an agency for sending messages or short reports. If your organization uses a particular memo format, then you should use it. If not, use white bond, 16- to 20-pound weight, 8 1/2 by 11 inch paper. Use 1 to 1 1/2 inch margins, single spacing within memo parts and double spacing between parts. Use block left-margin page format and center the memo vertically. (See Example 17.1.)

1. MEMO HEADINGS

The memo heading has four standard subheadings: DATE, TO, FROM, and SUBJECT. They can appear in any order, but TO and FROM are usually placed together. The subheadings are typed in all capital letters and in boldface type to make them clearly stand out. Each should be followed with a colon (:). All information in each line is aligned on the same vertical margin.

1.1 DATE

Use month, day, year (or day, month, year), and type out the name of the month to avoid misunderstanding.

1.2 TO

Use the recipient's first and last name (or first initials and last name if they prefer), and include the person's title or position. Use a second line if the title is long.

1.3 FROM

Type your name and include your title or position. Sign your initials, by hand, next to your name before sending the memo to indicate that you've signed it.

1.4 SUBJECT

Name the topic of your memo (i.e., Notice of New Vacation Schedule; Confirmation of Budget Meeting, Tues. July 9; Biodiversity Team 2 Weekly Report).

2. BODY

This is the text of your message. Single-space within paragraphs and double-space between them. Indenting first lines of paragraphs is optional, but do the same with every paragraph, whether you indent or not.

3. OPTIONAL MEMO PARTS

3.1 Reference Initials

If a typist prepared the memo, then the typist's initials appear in lowercase letters on the left margin, two spaces below the last paragraph.

3.2 Attachment Notice

Type the word "Attachment" on the left margin, two lines below the last line or notation on the memo, if you are including an attachment to the memo, such as another document.

Example 17.1 Sample Memo

Headings

DATE:	15 January 2002
TO:	Betty Morales, Chair, City College Art Department Lee Sakamoto, Dean, City College Humanities Division
FROM:	*AB* Anthony Blake, *City College Arts* Writer and Editor
SUBJECT:	*City College Arts*, Spring 2002 issue

Body

I know you are busy with this semester's classes, but it is already time to write the *City College Arts* spring issue. All material must be in before March 1 if it is going to be finished, printed, and distributed in time to announce the upcoming performances and shows. Please remind your instructors that, if they are in charge of a show or a performance that will be presented this spring, I need information about it for writing *City College Arts* within the next four weeks. Please note the Spring Arts Calendar attached and have them call me (x1144), e-mail me, or come by and see me. Thank you.

Notation

Attachment: Spring Arts Calendar

CHAPTER 18

E-Mail Format

1. E-Mail Headings and Icons
   1.1 To
   1.2 Copy (Cc)
   1.3 Subject
   1.4 Attachment

2. Message Box
   2.1 Salutation or Greeting
   2.2 Body
   2.3 Closing
   2.4 Writer's Name
   2.5 Attachment Icon(s)
3. A Note on Emoticons

Electronic mail (e-mail) is sent everywhere, within organizations and between them, as well as informally between individuals. Its format borrows elements from letters and memos. (See Figure 18.1.)

1. E-MAIL HEADINGS AND ICONS

E-mail headings usually have two or three standard subheadings and a variety of icons for optional information, the most common of which are: To, Cc, Subject, and an Attachment icon. They require that you simply fill in the blanks.

1.1 To

In most e-mail programs, you can type in a person's name or a company name and the e-mail address, or you can store e-mail addresses electronically in your "Address Book." With stored addresses, all you have to do is type part of the person's name and it will appear, or click on the **To** icon, then the **Address Book** icon, then click on the name that you want. When you click **OK** to your choice(s), it will automatically appear in the **To** line on your e-mail heading. It is important to get the person's e-mail address exactly right, otherwise it will not get delivered. However, you will receive a notice that it was not delivered. E-mail allows no errors in addresses, so check e-mail addresses carefully.

1.2 Copy (Cc:)

Depending on the e-mail program, **Copy** is on its own line or is an option with an icon. It is for sending a copy of your e-mail to a person other than the primary person listed in the **To** line. It works the same as filling in the **To** line.

1.3 Subject

Name the topic of your e-mail message. Be brief and as clear as possible (i.e., Roommate Search Ongoing, New Benefits Package Highlights, Weekend Plans). If you simply click the **Reply** icon to someone else's e-mail, the **Subject** line will automatically use their **Subject** line, but it will be preceded with a reference notation (**Re:**), such as, **Re:** Weekend Plans. Some people capitalize all major words in their subject line, like it's a title (which is good for more serious e-mails), but some capitalize only the first word and lower case all others (this is okay for personal e-mail).

1.4 Attachment

This is usually a paper clip icon. Clicking on this icon allows you to attach a file or files from your computer and send a file copy to the person receiving your e-mail. It is a great way to send documents, spreadsheets, etc.

Figure 18.1 Sample E-Mail

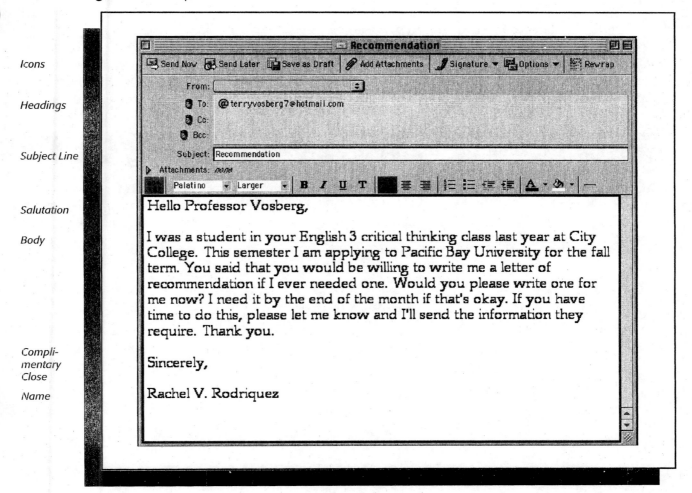

Icons

Headings

Subject Line

Salutation

Body

Compli-mentary Close

Name

---

2. MESSAGE BOX

This is for the text of your e-mail. Single-space within parts and double-space between each part.

2.1 Salutation or Greeting

Depending on the seriousness of your e-mail, this can be formal or informal (e.g., "Mr. Johnson," "Hi Sally," "Juan and Maria," "Hello").

2.2 Body

This is your message. Single-space within paragraphs and double-space between paragraphs. E-mail programs are becoming more sophisticated in their formatting, but check for limitations before you try to send anything with fancy formatting or fonts. Block style and a flush-left margin is the most commonly used page format. Use upper and lowercase letters. Don't use all capital letters; it is considered to be "shouting" and, therefore, impolite.

2.3 Closing

Generally, the closing is simple (e.g., "Thanks," "Regards," "Best," "Sincerely"). Choose what best fits your message.

2.4 Writer's Name

Type your name and title for formal correspondence; use two lines if necessary, or if it looks better to do so. Often, only first names are used with personal correspondence. Use what's appropriate.

2.5 Attachment Icon(s)

These icons indicate that an attachment, usually a file, is included in the e-mail. Clicking on the icon will usually give a choice between opening the attachment or saving it to disk.

3. A NOTE ON EMOTICONS

Emoticons are those symbols created by using different keys, such as :-) ;-) :-D :-o :-/ :-(:-|. Scores of these emoticons have been created and are used as abbreviations of emotions, thoughts, ideas, and so on. As a general rule, they are not used in formal correspondence, but they are widely used in personal messages. Use good judgment when considering using emoticons.

CHAPTER 19

Research: A Basic Approach

1. Research: A Basic Approach
2. Sources of Information
   2.1 General Sources
   2.2 Periodicals
   2.3 Specialized Periodical Indexes
   2.4 Other Printed Information
   2.5 Electronic and Online Databases
   2.6 The Internet
   2.7 Other Electronic Sources
   2.8 Personal Interviews
   2.9 Surveys
3. Collecting Information
   3.1 Bibliographic Information
   3.2 Taking Notes
   3.3 Photocopying
   3.4 Printouts
   3.5 Audio and Video Recordings
4. A General Rule

1. RESEARCH: A BASIC APPROACH

You'll often find that when you have to write a paper, do a report, or give a presentation, you must do some research. One seldom knows everything there is to know about a topic, and information seems to increase daily on all kinds of topics. Having complete and up-to-date information is important when discussing any worthwhile topic.

When you start your research, start with yourself. What do you know about the topic? Jot down a few notes. Not only will this help you get started, it will also give you an idea of what you need to know and what research you need to do.

Doing research basically means finding information. However, information comes in many different forms, including facts, statistics, case studies, historic records, personal experience, opinions, and quotes from experts. Any or all of these may be useful to you in your research.

2. SOURCES OF INFORMATION

Knowing where to find information is key to good research. There are innumerable sources of information, but they all fall into several basic categories.

2.1 General Sources

General sources include encyclopedias, dictionaries, almanacs and books of facts, general histories, references, and so on. These sources are good for obtaining general, basic information about people and topics, and they are a good place to start your research.

2.2 Periodicals

Periodicals include news magazines (e.g., *Time*), professional journals and newsletters (e.g., *Journal of the American Medical Association*), bulletins (e.g. *AARP Bulletin*), and newspapers (e.g., *The New York Times*). It

Figure 19.1 Sample Entries from *Readers' Guide to Periodical Literature*

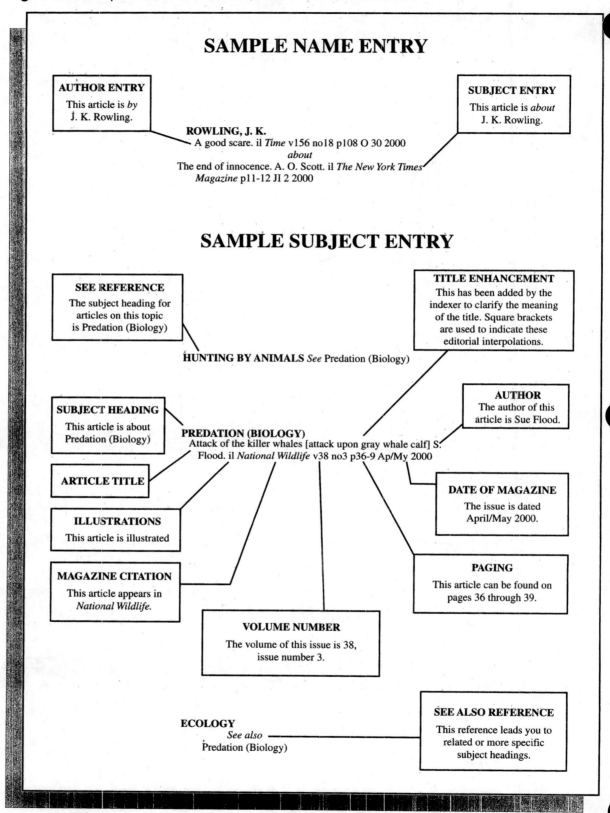

SAMPLE NAME ENTRY

AUTHOR ENTRY
This article is *by* J. K. Rowling.

SUBJECT ENTRY
This article is *about* J. K. Rowling.

ROWLING, J. K.
A good scare. il *Time* v156 no18 p108 O 30 2000
about
The end of innocence. A. O. Scott. il *The New York Times Magazine* p11-12 Jl 2 2000

SAMPLE SUBJECT ENTRY

SEE REFERENCE
The subject heading for articles on this topic is Predation (Biology)

TITLE ENHANCEMENT
This has been added by the indexer to clarify the meaning of the title. Square brackets are used to indicate these editorial interpolations.

HUNTING BY ANIMALS *See* Predation (Biology)

SUBJECT HEADING
This article is about Predation (Biology)

AUTHOR
The author of this article is Sue Flood.

PREDATION (BIOLOGY)
Attack of the killer whales [attack upon gray whale calf] S. Flood. il *National Wildlife* v38 no3 p36-9 Ap/My 2000

ARTICLE TITLE

DATE OF MAGAZINE
The issue is dated April/May 2000.

ILLUSTRATIONS
This article is illustrated

PAGING
This article can be found on pages 36 through 39.

MAGAZINE CITATION
This article appears in *National Wildlife*.

VOLUME NUMBER
The volume of this issue is 38, issue number 3.

ECOLOGY
See also
Predation (Biology)

SEE ALSO REFERENCE
This reference leads you to related or more specific subject headings.

Source: Readers' Guide to Periodical Literature (Nov. 2001, p. 154). Used by permission.

Figure 19.2 Human Cloning Entry from *The Readers' Guide to Periodical Literature,* Nov. 2001

HUMAN CLONING

Cloning: humans may have it easier. C. Gorman. il *Time* v158 no8 p56-7 Ag 27 2001

The God game no more [Clonaid, human cloning project formed by Raelians] N. Boyce and D. E. Kaplan. il por *U.S. News & World Report* v131 no2 p20-1 Jl 9-16 2001

It's a bird, it's a plane, it's–superclone? K. Pollitt. il *The Nation* v273 no4 p10 Jl 23-30 2001

Send in the clones? [stem cells and human cloning] il *U.S. News & World Report* v131 no7 p12 Ag 20-27 2001

Sex, errors, and the genome. M. Ridley. il *Natural History* v110 no5 p42-51 Je 2001

Ethical aspects

Ban stand [need to ban human cloning] L. R. Kass and D. Callahan. *The New Republic* v225 no6 p10-12 Ag 6 2001

'The heart of my mystery' [danger of human cloning is exaggerated] T. Dalrymple. *National Review* v53 no13 p37-9 Jl 9 2001

Human cloning: toward a brave new world. L. R. Kass. *Current* (Washington, D.C.) no4231 p9-19 Mr/Ap 2001

The rush to clone [cover story] T. A. Shannon. il *American* v185 no6 p8-10 S 10 2001

Shun cloning [views of R. Jaenisch and I. Wilmot] C. Murtaugh. *Commonweal* v128 no10 p9-10 My 18 2001

International aspects

The debate over human cloning. por *World Press Review* v48 no10 p5 O 2001

Laws and regulations

Ban stand [need to ban human cloning] L. R. Kass and D. Callahan. *The New Republic* v225 no6 p10-12 Ag 6 2001

Bush grapples with stem cells, cloning. G. Vogel. il *Science* v292 no 5526 p2409-11 Je 29 2001

Cloning bills proliferate in U.S. Congress. g. Vogel. il *Science* v292 no5519 p1037 My 11 2001

Cloning: where do you draw the line? [stem cell debate and House vote on human cloning] N. Gibbs. il *Time* v158 no 6 p18-21 Ag 13 2001

is most efficient if you use periodical indexes to look up topics of information for these sources. The *Reader's Guide to Periodical Literature* is an excellent index for English language journals and magazines. You can look up information by subject name(s) or by author(s) name(s). (See Figures 19.1 and 19.2)

Major newspapers, such as *The New York Times* and *The Los Angeles Times,* also have indexes for looking up articles they have published (e.g., *The New York Times Index*).

2.3 Specialized Periodical Indexes

These references are available for most general subject areas, such as agriculture, art, biology, education, engineering, humanities, law, science and technology, music, and so on. Consider the following partial list of indexes:

- Agricultural Index
- Art Index
- Biological Abstracts
- Education Index
- Engineering Index
- Humanities Index
- Index to Legal Periodicals
- Applied Science and Technology Index
- Music Index

2.4 Other Printed Information

This category includes newsletters, pamphlets, informational booklets, annual reports, government documents, the Congressional Record, dissertations, proceedings from a conference, letters, and graphics (e.g., charts, maps, graphs).

2.5 Electronic and Online Databases

These are electronic indexes or sources (some including full-text articles), such as DIALOG, BRS, ProQuest, EBSCOHOST, Infotrac, AskERIC, and so on. These indexes essentially work like search engines. By entering key words, you can search for titles or authors covering various subjects contained in the database.

2.6 The Internet

This includes the World Wide Web (WWW) and all other sources available online. (See Chapters 20 and 21.)

2.7 Other Electronic Sources

These include films and videotape (e.g., TV news magazines, PBS programs, documentaries), audiotape (e.g., speeches, sound recordings), CD-ROMs and DVDs.

2.8 Personal Interviews

Don't forget that other people can be great sources of information, especially those who are expert in their field. Ask knowledgeable people questions or request an interview with them. Most people are very helpful if you tell them you are doing research and want to talk to them. This is an excellent way to obtain some good information and perhaps a few quotes you can use.

2.9 Surveys

Asking many different people to respond to a series of questions can help you discover what they know about your topic and the aspects of your topic, or perhaps what misconceptions they might have, or what opinion they hold on your topic (e.g., "Do you favor human cloning to grow tissues and organs?"). Write up a short series of questions about your topic, starting with general questions, then proceeding to more specific questions and aspects about which people can express their knowledge and opinions. You may get some interesting information ("The survey found that 21 of 25 people thought human cloning should be regulated.").

3. COLLECTING INFORMATION

After you find the appropriate source of information, you need to collect what you find. As a general rule, save any piece of information that seems like it might be useful. It's always easier to toss out some bit of information that turns out not to be useful than to try to remember it and find it again. Collect first, sort later.

3.1 Bibliographic Information

When you collect information, no matter which method you use, record and keep all of the following bibliographic information for each source:

- Author(s) name(s)
- Title of the book or article or source
- City of publication
- Name of publisher
- Edition number, volume number, etc.
- Date of publication or update
- Page numbers
- URL (if an electronic source)
- Date of access (if an electronic source)
- Any other publication information that seems important

You will often be required to supply this information with your research so that others can see exactly what your sources of information were, so they can also refer to them if they wish.

The important thing about collecting information is to be absolutely accurate and to make sure not to change the meaning or intent of the information.

3.2 Taking Notes

Some people prefer to write out the research information they find. They may write the information directly, quoting it word for word; they may paraphrase (reword, usually to shorten) the information; or they may summarize (condense to main points, ideas, etc.) the information. This process can be tedious, but the advantage of taking notes is that it helps you to better learn and retain the information.

3.3 Photocopying

A fast way to collect information is to photocopy the information and articles you find. However, take care not to miss any pages or bibliographic information. The advantage of this method is speed. The disadvantage is cost; it can become expensive very quickly. Scan the information first to be sure you want it before you run up a bill for photocopy charges.

3.4 Printouts

Most electronic databases and Internet sources allow you the ability to download or print out information you find. The obvious advantage of this method is speed. The disadvantage is that in libraries with access to these databases and the Internet, there is often a fee for printing the information you want to collect. With Internet-based sources and databases, usually you can copy and e-mail the information to yourself and print it later at home without copying costs.

3.5 Audio and Video Recordings

When interviewing people, you may want to record your interview on audiotape, disk, or video. Always ask permission first before recording someone electronically. There may also be times when you might want to read information into an audio recorder, or you might want to videotape information, especially if it's basically visual information.

Realize that recorded information may be no more reliable than printed information. Take the time to double-check and verify the accuracy and truthfulness of your information.

4. A GENERAL RULE

When doing research, try to find and collect all the necessary information for a thorough and intelligent discussion of your topic and to make your point. Don't be too concerned about how much information to collect. It is usually wise to collect more information than you need because some information will appear in more than one source (often in several), and some information may not be useful for the particular aspect of your topic that you're discussing. That's the nature of good research. Collect lots of information—with practice, you'll be able to more accurately judge when you have all the information you need. One thing that most people discover is that doing research teaches you how to do it better. With practice, the entire process becomes easier and more natural.

Exercises

1. Find at least four sources of information for each of the following and record the bibliographic information for each source.

   • Air marshals
   • Flat tax initiatives

- In vitro fertilization
- The Napster lawsuit
- Operation Enduring Freedom

2. Alternate list: Find at least four sources of information for each of the following and record the bibliographic information for each source.

- The baseball career of Mark McGuire
- Henry VIII and his wives
- The human genome project
- Three Strikes law
- The writings of William Faulkner

3. Collect research notes and information on one of the selections from Number 1 or 2 above and bring in the information for class or group discussion.

CHAPTER 20

Research and Browsing on the Internet

1. Internet Research
    1.1 Internet URLs
    1.2 World Wide Web
    1.3 Search Engines
    1.4 Some Useful Search Engines
    1.5 Searching by Category
    1.6 Searching by Keyword(s)

1. INTERNET RESEARCH

1.1 Internet URLs

Each Internet site and page has an electronic address known as a Uniform Resource Locator (URL), for example, *http://www.excite.com*. The URL appears near the top of the page, and is usually called Location, Netsite, or something similar. By clicking on the URL, it can be changed to any address you want to visit.

1.2 World Wide Web

There are several servers on the Internet, but the most commonly used is probably the World Wide Web (WWW or the Web). It allows your **browser** to navigate quickly through the millions of **hypertext** sites that contain the information and images you are searching when you do research online.

The Web now contains over a billion pages and has hundreds of millions of images that you can access. About 75 percent of the Internet has commercial content; the remainder is scientific, educational, nonprofit organizations, government, and so on.

1.3 Search Engines

Search engines are programs that allow access to Internet sites by using keyword searches. Click **Search** at the top of your browser's home page for a list of search engines.

1.4 Some Useful Search Engines

The following are some search engines that you may find useful when doing research online.

AllTheWeb.com *http://www.alltheweb.com/*
(also known as FAST Search; a very large index)
Alta Vista *http://www.altavista.com/*
(one of the most comprehensive)
AOL Search *http://search.aol.com/*
(across the Web for AOL members)
Ask Jeeves *http://www.askjeeves.com/*
(attempts to go to exact page to answer questions)
Excite *http://www.excite.com/*
(good at ranking the relevance of a site and suggesting similar sites)
Hot Bot *http://hotbot.lycos.com/*
(allows customized searches)
Infoseek *http://infoseek.go.com/*
(one of the most accurate; allows searches of results of a previous search)
LookSmart *http://www.looksmart.com/*
(partnered with MSN Search, Excite, and others)

Lycos *http://www.lycos.com/*
(allows advanced search features)
Yahoo! *http://www.yahoo.com/*
(has a very detailed subject directory)

Meta (multi) search engines list several search engine results at once.

Dogpile *http://www.dogpile.com/*
Google *http://www.google.com/*
iSleuth *http://www.isleuth.com/*
Metacrawler *http://www.metacrawler.com/*
ProFusion *http://www.profusion.com/*
Search.com *http://www.search.com/*
WebCrawler *http://www.webcrawler.com/*

5. Searching by Category

Many search engines have subject directories that list Internet sites under categories. Searching by category allows you to limit your results to subjects most relevant to your topic (**Arts and Humanities**, **Business and Economy**, **Computers and Internet**, **Education**, etc.). Each category usually is further divided into subcategories.

6. Searching by Keyword(s)

Searching by keyword(s) will result in lots of information, much of which may not be relevant to your topic. Remember: (1) Keep keywords specific, and (2) Check spelling.

To refine your keyword search:

- Use **AND** to connect words that need to be found together: Capital **AND** punishment. Without **AND** you'll get thousands of listings that only refer to "capital" and thousands that refer to "punishment" (of any kind) mixed in with the listings for "capital punishment." *Note:* Some search engines use a comma instead of **AND**; some use a plus (+) sign before necessary words.

- Use **NOT** before words that must not come up in the search: Cloning **NOT** human. With **NOT** you will be able to find all the information you want about "cloning" without also receiving listings about "cloning human beings." NOTE: Some search engines use a minus (−) sign to exclude words from the search.

- Use **OR** if only one of the keywords must be found in the search: Elk **OR** Wapiti. With **OR**, you expand your search, in this case by including "wapiti," which is an American Indian word often used for "elk."

- Use **quotation marks** ("") around keywords that are part of a phrase: "search engines." Using quotation marks will tell the search that these words must appear together.

- Use an **asterisk** (*) to indicate letters that may vary because of plurals, suffixes, and so on: "business manag*" Using the asterisk will allow a broad search that would find several related topics at once (in this case, business management, business managing, business managers, etc.).

CHAPTER 21

Evaluating the Credibility of Internet Sites and Information Sources

1. Some Points to Consider
   1.1 Sites
   1.2 Author(s)
   1.3 Accuracy
   1.4 Currency
   1.5 Objectivity
   1.6 Credibility

.1. SOME POINTS TO CONSIDER

Remember, just because information appears or is published on the Internet doesn't mean that it is accurate, authoritative, or reliable. Whereas information that appears in newspapers, journals, references, TV news, library collections, and similar sources is usually reviewed, checked, and evaluated, anyone may publish anything on the Internet, without verification of facts. Just as all printed and media information should be evaluated for accuracy and objectivity, all Internet sites and authors should be evaluated as well.

1.1 Sites

- What is the site's domain? Look at the URL to check the site's domain name (e.g., **.com**, commercial; **.edu**, educational; **.gov**, governmental; **.mil**, military; **.net**, network; **.org**, nonprofit organizations; **.biz**, business).
- Who publishes the site? What are their credentials or qualifications?
- Does the site have a sponsor or supporting organization behind it?
- What is the scope of the site and its information? What is included and what isn't?
- Is the site mostly images or is there a balance between images and text information?
- Does the site have links to other related sites and information?
- Is it possible to make contact by e-mail, fax, phone, or "snail" mail?

1.2 Author(s)

- Is an author listed? Check the beginning and the end of the site (including its pages and its documents) because the author(s) may be listed in either place.
- What are the author's credentials, qualifications, educational background, expertise, and/or experience?
- Is it possible to contact the author by e-mail, fax, phone, or "snail" mail?

1.3 Accuracy

- Does the site seem to contain accurate information and facts?
- Is the information presented error-free? If so, it indicates that the site has been reviewed or edited, and is probably professional.

1.4 Currency

- Does the site have a current publication or upload date?
- Does the page or information have a current publication or upload date?
- Are links updated and current?

1.5 Objectivity

- What subjects and material are covered? Are the viewpoints presented reasonable and balanced? Do they appear to be well-researched?
- Are there any signs of bias in the tone, language, images, and so on?
- Does the site or author have any political, social, or religious leanings or agenda?
- Is the site or author affiliated with a special-interest group (e.g., NRA, ACLU, Planned Parenthood, NOW, Sierra Club)?
- How detailed is the site and information? Are any claims supported with sufficient and relevant evidence? Is there sufficient and proper documentation?
- How does the site or author treat opposing views? Fairly? Reasonably?
- How does the site and information compare with other similar sites?

1.6 Credibility

Learning to objectively evaluate Internet sites and sources will help you do research more efficiently and give credibility to your documents.

CHAPTER 22
Writing Research Papers

1. Research Papers: A Basic Approach
2. Preparation
   2.1 Choosing a Topic
   2.2 Doing Preliminary Reading
   2.3 Creating a Thesis: Taking a Position
   2.4 Making a Scratch Outline
   2.5 Finding Sources for Specific Information
   2.6 Recording Bibliographic Information
2.7 Collecting Information
2.8 Finalizing Your Thesis
2.9 Organizing Your Paper
   2.9.1 Editing
   2.9.2 Grouping
   2.9.3 Outlining
3. Writing and Revising
   3.1 Writing a Draft
   3.2 Doing Revision
   3.3 Proofreading and Printing

1. RESEARCH PAPERS: A BASIC APPROACH

Writing a research paper can be a major undertaking, but it need not be so daunting if you follow a carefully laid out process. This process will take time and significant effort to research and write a good paper, but following a basic, well-thought-out plan will make the task much easier and will lead to better results.

2. PREPARATION

2.1 Choosing a Topic

If a topic has not been assigned to you, then you must choose one. It is important that the topic fit the assignment given to you. Also you should make the topic specific; that is, limit it. "Health care" is too broad a topic; it would require an entire book. Choose something more specific, such as "HMOs" or "genetic engineering." Then narrow your topic to a specific aspect that you can adequately cover in a standard-length essay or research paper (usually 6 to 10 pages, typed or word processed), such as "HMO regulation" or "the ethics of genetic testing."

2.2 Doing Preliminary Reading

You may not know much about your topic, but that's okay. That's what research is for—to gather information and learned about a specific topic so you can become informed and then intelligently discuss the topic. Begin by checking general sources—basic library references—such as almanacs, encyclopedias, atlases, books of facts, and so on. Remember, your most important sources of information in the library are the reference librarians. Finding information is their area of expertise. If you don't know where to look, just ask; they'll be pleased to help you. Find and read enough information to familiarize yourself with your topic so that you understand the basics and any major points of argument or contention involving the topic.

2.3 Creating a Thesis: Taking a Position

Create a preliminary thesis. Most research papers require that you take a position on whatever topic you've decided to discuss. Simply decide if you want to be for or against your topic; for example, that something should be legal or illegal. For instance, you may decide that HMOs need stricter government regulation, or that genetic testing without consent should be illegal. Write your thesis in one direct sentence; for example, "HMOs should be more strictly regulated by the federal government" or "Genetic testing should be illegal." This approach will help guide your in-depth research. Don't be overly concerned about taking the "right" position on your topic. Most college instructors are interested in the quality of your research, the strength of your argument, and your overall written presentation, not your position on the topic. It's more important that your thesis be clear and well-supported with research and sound reasoning. Later you may find that you'll modify or change your thesis as necessary to more closely fit your research findings, but start with a short, concise thesis sentence. It will help direct your research and help in planning your paper.

2.4 Making a Scratch Outline

Once you've decided on your position on your topic, it is helpful to make a brief outline of the major points or reasons that support your thesis. Typically, a research paper may touch on points such as feasibility, efficiency, legality, morality/religion, cost, and so on. List your major points or reasons in scratch outline form. Doing so will also greatly help to guide your in-depth research into your topic. You will know what kind of information you need to look for, which will make your search more efficient and less time consuming.

EXAMPLE: SAMPLE SCRATCH OUTLINE

Topic/Thesis: *Opposing Internet Censorship in Libraries*
1. *First Amendment/freedom of speech*
2. *Court cases and rulings*
3. *Blocking software problems*
4. *Blocked sites*
5. *Libraries and Internet access*
6. *Alternatives to blocking software*

2.5 Finding Sources for Specific Information

In-depth research requires extensive searching of information sources. You must look into computerized card catalogues, check newspaper and periodical (magazine and journal) indexes, search major subject and specialized indexes, and go online to use Internet search engines. Use your thesis to guide you and do keyword searches to find more in-depth information about your topic. Don't neglect using people as a resource in your research. Conduct an interview with someone knowledgeable in the aspects of your topic, or conduct a survey to gather information, opinions, quotes, and so on. For example, you could interview a nurse or a doctor about their view of HMOs. Most professionals will be happy to help you out.

2.6 Recording Bibliographic Information

Often you will be required to supply bibliographic details about the sources of information that you use. Such details may include name of the author(s), title(s), city of publication, name of publisher, edition, date of publication or update, page numbers, URL and date of access, (if an Internet source), and so on. Collect as much of these data as possible from every source that you use, whether a book, magazine, Web site, or whatever. Record these details when you get information from any source, otherwise you won't be able to properly document your research paper. Having this information will also help you to avoid plagiarism (see Chapter 23).

2.7 Collecting Information

When you find useful information, take notes or photocopy it or record it in some way. If the information is from an electronic source or the Internet, download and print out the material. Collect any facts, data, ideas, concepts, opinions, quotes, and so on that are relevant or useful to supporting your thesis. You can sort the information later. Try to verify the validity of the information you gather. Check it against other sources. Do your best to see that the information is reasonable, accurate, and logical (review Chapters 19–21).

2.8 Finalizing Your Thesis

After you've completed your research, you should finalize your thesis and make it as clear and straightforward as possible. During the course of your research you may have discovered things you didn't know about your topic and you may have changed your mind on your initial position. If so, that's okay. Research is supposed to help us make informed decisions. However, if your position or opinion has changed, now is the time to modify your thesis to match your new thinking. Rewrite your thesis in one clear, concise sentence, for example, "Human genetic testing without consent should be illegal." Your rewritten thesis will now guide you through your research paper writing.

2.9 Organizing Your Paper

To effectively discuss any topic, the topic must be logically and clearly presented. The information must be organized so it will make sense and be easy for readers to follow. If necessary, rearrange or expand your scratch outline to help you organize your thoughts. Arrange the main points in the order in which you wish to discuss them.

2.9.1 *Editing*

As with any writing project, you should edit the information you are going to use. You probably will have collected more information than you need for your paper. Look at what you have gathered and decide what information will be useful—keep this and discard or ignore the rest. If you aren't sure of a piece of information's usefulness, keep it for the time being; you can use it or discard it later.

2.9.2 *Grouping*

Organize the information that you decide to use into groups, placing related information together. You can use your outline's major points as your major group categories. Put your research information into the appropriate group, whether facts, data, quotes, case studies, examples, and so on. All of your useful information should fall into a group listed in your outline.

2.9.3 *Outlining*

If you are working on a complex topic or one with a lot of information, it may help you to revise and expand your scratch outline. Simply determine whether your scratch outline is complete and your major points are in the order you want. Then subdivide any of the major points necessary to accommodate and clarify the information you wish to use to discuss that point. For example, if you are making a point about a topic's feasibility and you need to discuss time and money, you could discuss these aspects as two subpoints under the general discussion point of feasibility. Make your expanded outline reflect your research information and your plan of presentation. As long as your outline has a place for all of your information and follows a logical progression, it will be useful as a framework to write your research paper.

Exercises and Discussion Questions

1. Choose a topic for a research paper, then narrow it down (e.g., "cloning" narrowed down to "cloning humans"). After some preliminary research and reading, pick a position on your topic (for or against) and write a thesis statement for your research paper (e.g., "Human cloning should be illegal.").
2. Individually or in groups, narrow down each of the following general topics for a possible research paper topic, then write a thesis statement for the narrowed topic. Compare yours with those of other students.

- ACT/SAT testing
- Bilingual education
- Censorship
- Genetic engineering
- Handgun possession
- Health maintenance organizations (HMOs)
- Homelessness
- Immigration
- The Internet
- Terrorism
- Welfare

3. WRITING AND REVISING

If you are writing a classic argumentative research paper on a controversial issue, refer to the Appendix for help with outlining the structure of your paper.

3.1 Writing a Draft

Your goal in writing a first draft is to get all your information down on paper or in the computer in the order you want. Follow the basic paper-writing process and your outline. Simply transcribe your thoughts on your main points, followed by research (e.g., facts, data, quotes, examples) to back up each point, until all the points have been discussed and supported with research information. In the first draft, your goal is to get everything down on paper. Don't stop to correct spelling, punctuation, grammar, and so on. Doing so will only slow you down and frustrate you. There's time for fine-tuning later.

If your paper is long or complex, you may not be able to complete the first draft in one sitting. In that case, just work on writing a section at a time and do not try to finish the entire paper at once. Let each major point be a section. It usually works best if you try to do an entire section at one time, because it is easier to maintain the flow of information if you don't break your train of thought.

Although it is not necessary to complete the sections in order, for most people it is more logical to do so. For example, if you feel more comfortable writing the shorter sections first and working up to the longer ones, then do so, but don't forget to add transitions later to smooth the flow of your paper. Don't worry about getting the introduction perfect or fine tuning the conclusion in your first draft. Concentrate on the information—just include everything that needs to be said to start with, as best you can on a first try, in the order that you planned.

3.2 Doing Revision

Of course, some revision and rewriting will be necessary to improve your rough draft. However, if you've spent sufficient time planning, researching, and organizing, this should not be an endless task. It should primarily consist of refining and polishing your information and writing. Revision should concentrate on content and writing style, not spelling, mechanics, grammar, and so on. First, check to see that you've said what you wanted to say, in the way you wanted to say it, and in the order you wanted. Make sure that nothing has been left out and that there are no holes in the information, logic, or flow of the language. If you find that something is missing (e.g., another fact or piece of information), find it and insert it in the appropriate place. Also check to see that no unnecessary information slipped in. If so, remove it. Ensure that your presentation of information is clear and logical, and progresses smoothly throughout your paper. Check that your writing (the language) flows naturally and clearly. Fine-tune or rephrase any sentences that don't flow smoothly. Remember, to be persuasive, you must be understood; to be understood, your writing should be as clear and easy to follow as possible. Strive for clarity, not perfection; clarity is obtainable, perfection is not. Revise as you think necessary, but keep your deadline in mind.

Be sure to follow the format requirements given, especially when doing your last revision. Ensure that all required parts, sections, and pages are included in the required order.

You might consider discussing your revision with your instructor or a tutor, if possible. You might ask your roommate, a classmate, or your spouse to look over your paper to see if everything is clear and complete.

3.3 Proofreading and Printing

When you've finished your revisions, it is time to check grammar, spelling, punctuation, and so on. Read through your paper slowly and deliberately, not for what it says, but to check the high standards to which good writing must adhere and which research papers require.

Use a college style manual to check grammar (e.g., word usage, verbs) and punctuation. You can use the grammar checker in a word-processing program, but be wary. Most are fairly accurate, but the sentence construction suggestions they offer, while usually technically correct, often tend to make your language sound stiff, stilted, and mechanical. You want your writing to be grammatically correct, but you also want to sound human. It's better if you make your own corrections and maintain the language that makes your writing style your own. Use a style guide and refer to it to check your punctuation as well. Use a dictionary or spellchecker, too. However, be wary of spellcheckers as not all are reliable. When you've checked everything as carefully as you can, it's time to make corrections and do your final draft. Check everything one last time, then print your finished paper. It should look good after all the work you have put into it.

Refer to the sample research paper that follows (Example 22.1).

Example 22.1 Sample Formal Research Paper

Formal Cover Page

Internet Filtering Software
in Public Libraries

By
Jared Martinez

English 3H
Professor C. D. Rooks
February 20, 2002

Martinez 1

Introduction of Issue

The Internet has quickly become one of the most valuable information resources available. With today's technological advances, anyone can access almost any type of information at the click of a button. In public libraries and elsewhere, Internet access provides an excellent supplement to traditional research tools. Nevertheless, a growing concern is the ability for children to access pornographic material while in the library. Internet filtering software that blocks access to Web sites based on content has grown to be a popular consideration.

Positions People Take

Some people feel libraries that provide unfiltered Internet access aid access to Internet pornography. Others believe that Internet content is protected by the First Amendment, which guarantees free speech, and believe it is the parents' role to monitor children's Internet viewing.

Historic and Background Information

The U.S. Supreme Court has not been totally clear on the matter of indecency, obscenity, and pornography. In Roth v. United States (1957), Justice William Brennan wrote ". . . [obscenity is not] within the area of constitutionally protected speech or press." This would seem to have settled the issue, but the problem lies in how "indecent" or "obscenity" is defined.

To confuse the issue further, in a later ruling, Chief Justice Warren C. Burger wrote in Miller v. California (1973): ". . . powers of the States do not vary from community to community, but this does not mean that they are, or should or can be, fixed, uniform national standards of what appeals to the 'prurient interest' or is 'patently offensive.'"

In essence, this means obscenity can be loosely defined under a community standards test. The problem remains: How is it possible to filter the Internet without a clear definition of what is obscene?

More Recent Background Information

In 1996, the U.S. Congress weighed in and passed the Communications Decency Act (CDA), which made distributing "indecent" material over the Internet illegal, but the U.S. Supreme Court struck down the law in 1997, declaring that the CDA was too vaguely worded and suppressed adult speech (Baird and Rosenbaum 59).

Thesis

Public schools and libraries should not use Internet filtering software because they are governmental institutions subject to the First Amendment.

Point/Reason #1

Internet filtering software should not be used because the software itself is based on vaguely defined and subjectively applied words and terms. Net Nanny, a popular brand of filtering software, has a list of words that, if found on a Web page, are blocked from access, in addition to Web sites that are not rated. In the process, access has been

Supporting Information

blocked to Web pages of the AIDS Quilt, Carnegie Mellon Banned Books, The Heritage Foundation, The American Association of University Women, and The Religious Society

Martinez 2

of Friends (the Quakers) (Hunter 77). What then occurs when a high school student is trying to research breast cancer for a science report? Never should an opportunity arise that a topic cannot be researched because a word in the subject can be interpreted, in some areas, as pornographic. Never should anyone feel limited as to what they can learn, know, and research because of an Internet filtering software company's bias toward certain issues. The question remains: How exactly do makers of Internet filtering software define what is on the "dirty words" list and what is not? For instance, Cyber Sitter software made it impossible for computers to access the homepages of the National Organization of Women (NOW). Its parent company, Solid Oak Software, admits to working closely with Focus on the Family, a conservative organization that has initiated campaigns against offensive books in public schools and libraries. Consequently, Cyber Sitter extends [this conservative] agenda (Cothran et al. 122).

More Supporting Information

In addition, why do supporters of Internet filtering software focus solely on Internet pornography when such material can be accessed via other mediums? Couldn't children just as easily view similar pornographic images while channel surfing through HBO, Showtime, or Cinemax? Internet filtering software activists act as if free speech and the First Amendment are a new concept when presented through a different medium such as the Internet (Cothran et al. 113). It is difficult to imagine that a child would be permanently injured by some chance encounters with "misrated" pornography any more than encountering it on cable television (Bernstein 1). Supporters of Internet filtering software argue that libraries are becoming pornographic meccas (Cothran et al. 128). In his article "X-Rated Libraries," Mark Y. Herring argues:

Point/Reason #2

Supporting Information

Counterpoint and Quote

> . . . 45 percent of all Internet pornography obtained through libraries [is] being accessed by underage people. Since libraries now offer 50 percent of all Internet access outside the home, they are fast becoming America's chief purveyors of pornography (26).

However, Herring does not cite a source for the aforementioned statistic. Is it valid? Is it representative of the population as a whole? These questions should be asked before accepting Herring's claim that 45 percent of people who access Internet pornography in libraries are underage.

Rebuttal

Government institutions such as public libraries and schools should not use Internet filtering software because there are other equally effective alternatives, such as the creation of child-friendly rooms in libraries and schools, monitored by librarians and

Point/Reason #3

Martinez 3

Supporting Argument

teachers. The formation of such rooms would not filter what adults could access and would provide a safe environment for children. Moreover, the establishment of an acceptable-use policy, with clear standards to which the user must sign and adhere, is another possible alternative. Such policies are already used in many public school districts, colleges, and libraries. With such policies, patrons will be deterred from accessing pornography at a public computer terminal. These methods would provide fair access to those who are entitled and still be enough of a safeguard for children to use the Internet as a learning tool.

Conclusion

It is the duty of libraries to promote free speech, a goal attained by providing access to free books and other instructional media, regardless of age or income. Using Internet filtering software over which schools and librarians have no control will inevitably block access to a wide range of constitutionally protected speech.

The definition of "obscenity" relies on community standards and is not consistent throughout the nation, as stated in <u>Miller v. California</u> (1973). Until one can define what is and what is not obscene, it is our duty to keep Internet filtering software out of institutions bound by our constitutional guarantee of free speech.

Martinez 4

Works Cited

An alphabetical listing of research materials used or directly quoted in the text of the paper.

Baird, Robert M., and Stuart E. Rosenbaum. <u>Pornography: Private Right or Public Menace</u>?. Amherst, MA: Prometheus, 1998.

Bernstein, Solvieg. "Beyond the Communications Decency Act: Constitutional Lessons of the Internet." <u>Cato Policy Analysis Online</u>. Cato Policy Analysis No. 262. 4 November 1996. 16 February 2002. ⟨http://www.cato.org/pubs/pas/pa-262.html⟩.

Cothran, Helen, et al. <u>Opposing Viewpoints: Pornography</u>. San Diego: Greenhaven, 2002.

Herring, Mark Y. "X-Rated Libraries." <u>Weekly Standard</u> 5 July 1999: 24–29.

Hunter, Christopher D. "Filtering the Future? Software Filters, Porn, Pics, and the Internet Content Conundrum." Diss. University of Pennsylvania, 1999.

<u>Miller v. California</u>. 413 U.S. 15. 1973.

<u>Roth v. United States</u>. 354 U.S. 476. 1957.

Part V

DOCUMENTATION

CHAPTER 23

Documentation and Plagiarism

1. Documentation	3. Documentation Styles
2. A Note on Plagiarism	

1. DOCUMENTATION

Often, written work and other assignments will involve gathering information through research. Some of that information will go into your paper or report. When you use that information, you must provide documentation by **citing** the source of the information as well as its author. Doing so gives the information credibility and strengthens the point you are making by telling the source of the information and giving credit to those from whom you borrowed the information.

Exception: The only time you don't have to cite a source is if the information is considered "common knowledge," something anyone should know, such as the Earth revolves around the sun or George W. Bush is the President of the United States.

Documentation is a formal method for giving people credit for their work and words, and the ideas, insights, and concepts within them. This practice is standard and expected in college classes and by all professionals. It is not difficult to do once learned, but it requires careful attention to the sources of your information.

2. A NOTE ON PLAGIARISM

From the time we are small children, we are taught not to take or borrow what belongs to other people without their permission. To do so is considered stealing. **Plagiarism** is a form of stealing. It is theft not of physical property but of intellectual property.

Ideas that people produce with their intellect, through thinking, are just as valuable as tangible things produced by hand; sometimes such ideas are more valuable. Such information, whether written or recorded by other means, "belongs" to the person who produced it. It is that person's intellectual property. When we use other people's work or words, we must give them credit. It is only fair that we do so. It would not be fair to take credit for work that is not our own. Besides, using proper documentation shows a level of skill, maturity, and sophistication in your written work that is highly regarded by all professionals.

NOTE: Penalties for plagiarism can be severe, and may include failing the course or losing your job. Document your sources carefully. It does not matter if you quoted the information directly or merely paraphrased it—you still must give credit. You are citing other people's information (ideas, insights, etc.), not simply their wording. So, acknowledge all your sources of information by citing and documenting each one.

3. DOCUMENTATION STYLES

Several documentation styles exist for citing sources of information. The style you use depends on whether you are working in the sciences, the humanities, or some other field. However, the two most common forms of documentation used in college courses are Modern Language Association (MLA) and American Psychological Association (APA). Both use in-text citation styles and bibliographic references (see Chapters 24 and 25, respectively.)

CHAPTER 24

MLA Documentation Style

1. In-Text Citations	2. Works Cited List
	2.1 Guidelines for MLA Works Cited
	2.2 Basic Elements for Works Cited Lists

When using information gathered from research, you *must* document your sources. Whether the information you use is quoted, paraphrased, or summarized, if it is not common knowledge, then you must cite your sources. The basic documentation style of the Modern Language Association (MLA) is shown below. For more detailed information on MLA style, consult the *MLA Handbook for Writers of Research Papers* (5th ed., 1999), the *MLA Style Manual* (2nd ed., 1998), or the MLA Web site (http://www.mla.org).

1. IN-TEXT CITATIONS

The MLA uses in-text citations rather than footnotes or endnotes to cite sources. The citation requires two pieces of information: (1) author's name (or, if no author, the article title in quotation marks) and (2) the page number(s) where the information was found. The author(s) may be mentioned in the text material along with the information or named after the information is given (last names only) inside parentheses with the page number(s).

EXAMPLES: IN-TEXT CITATIONS

Name(s) mentioned in text material; page number(s) at the end:

> According to researchers Michael Grubb and Niels Meyer, "migrating waterfowl . . . often change course at a great distance from wind turbines, and species that once fed in the vicinity of a windfarm apparently adapt rapidly to the presence of wind turbines and learn to avoid the rotors" (173).

> Chiles reports that the electrical output of one nuclear power plant is about 1,000 megawatts (54–55).

Name(s) given after the information; page number(s) at end:

> "Migrating waterfowl . . . often change course at a great distance from wind turbines, and species that once fed in the vicinity of a windfarm apparently adapt rapidly to the presence of wind turbines and learn to avoid the rotors" (Grubb and Meyer 173).

> The electrical output of one nuclear power plant is about 1,000 megawatts (Chiles 54–55).

2. WORKS CITED LIST

At the end of your paper, the sources of information that you used are listed with complete publication information. This list is called **Works Cited.** It lists your sources, *alphabetically,* by author's (or editor's) last name (or, if no author, by first word in the article title, but not *a, an,* or *the*). List only the sources you actually used and cited in your paper, not everything you researched and read (unless your instructor requires you to list all sources consulted).

EXAMPLES: WORKS CITED LISTING

Works Cited listing for in-text citations (p. 83):

> Chiles, James. "A Second Wind." <u>Smithsonian</u> Mar. 2000: 54–58.
> Grubb, Michael, and Niels Meyer. "Wind Energy: Resources, Systems, and Regional Strategies."
> <u>Renewable Energy: Sources for Fuels and Electricity</u>. Eds. Thomas B. Johansson, et al.
> Washington: Island, 1993. 167–189.

2.1 Guidelines for MLA Works Cited

- The Works Cited list should begin on a separate page at the end of the paper.
- The words Works Cited should be centered one inch from the top of the page.
- Do not put the words Works Cited in quotation marks or italics, or spell them with all capital letters.
- List sources alphabetically, not in the order you cited the sources in the paper.
- Begin every listing at the left-hand margin. If the information runs more than one line, indent each line after the first.
- Double-space all listings throughout the list.
- Do not number the listings.

Basic formats for the most common Works Cited listings follow the directory, Figure 24.1, below.

Figure 24.1 MLA Works Cited Listings Directory

Directory for MLA Works Cited Listings

Books

1. One Author
2. Edition Other Than First
3. Two or Three Authors
4. Four or More Authors
5. Corporate Author or Organization
6. No Author or Unknown Author
7. Two or More Books by Same Author(s)
8. Editor(s)
9. Translation
10. Anthology or Compilation
11. Selection from an Anthology
12. Reference Work: Encyclopedia or Dictionary
13. Multivolume Work
14. Book in a Series
15. Bible
16. Introduction, Preface, Forward, or Afterword

Periodicals

17. Article in a Weekly
18. Article in a Monthly
19. Article in a Newspaper
20. Article in a Journal Paginated by Issue
21. Article in a Journal Paginated by Volume
22. Editorial
23. Unsigned Article
24. Letter to the Editor
25. Review
26. A Special Issue

Other Sources (non-electronic)

27. Government Publication
28. Pamphlet
29. Published Interview
30. Personal Interview
31. Radio or Television Program
32. Radio or Television Interview

(*continued*)

33. Film or Video
34. Live Performance (Play, Opera, Ballet, Concert)
35. Musical Composition
36. Personal Letter or Memo
37. Published Letter
38. Lecture or Personal Address (Speech, Sermon, Reading)
39. Published Dissertation
40. Unpublished Dissertation
41. Dissertation Abstract
42. Proceedings of a Conference
43. Sound Recording
44. An Advertisement
45. Legal Source
46. Work of Art
47. Cartoon
48. Map or Chart

Electronic Sources

49. Online Scholarly Project or Information Database
50. Document in an Online Scholarly Project or Information Database
51. Personal or Professional Site
52. Online Book or Text
53. Article in an Online Periodical—Magazine or Journal
54. Article in an Online Periodical—Newspaper or Newswire
55. Publication on a CD-ROM, Diskette, or Magnetic Tape
56. Email Communication
57. Online Posting
58. Work from an Online Subscription Source
59. Synchronous Communication
60. Other Online Sources

2.2 Basic Elements for Works Cited Lists

Books

Author's last name, first name. <u>Book Title</u>. City of Publication: Publisher, Year of publication.
(*Note:* All other listings for books are variations of this basic format.)

1. One Author

Hawking, Stephen. <u>A Brief History of Time</u>. New York: Bantam, 1988.

2. Edition Other Than First

Rosenberg, Donna. <u>World Mythology</u>. 3rd ed. Lincolnwood, IL: NTC/Contemporary, 1999.

3. Two or Three Authors

McDonald, Daniel, and Larry W. Burton. <u>The Language of Argument</u>. 10th ed. New York: Longman, 2002.

4. Four or More Authors

Comley, Nancy R., et al. <u>Fields of Reading</u>. 6th ed. Boston: Bedford/St.Martin's, 2001.

5. Corporate Author or Organization

Bank of America. <u>Facts About Personal Deposit Account Programs</u>. San Francisco: Bank of America, 2000.

6. No Author or Unknown Author

<u>English Fairy Tales</u>. Hertfordshire, England: Wordsworth Editions Ltd., 1994.

7. Two or More Books by Same Author(s)

Eiseley, Loren. <u>The Star Thrower</u>. New York: Harcourt Brace, 1978.

— — —. <u>The Unexpected Universe</u>. New York: Harcourt Brace, 1969.

8. Editor(s)

Bennett, William J., ed. <u>The Moral Compass</u>. New York: Simon & Schuster, 1995.

9. Translation
Marquez, Gabriel Garcia. <u>One Hundred Years of Solitude</u>. Trans. Gregory Rabassa. New York: Bard-Avon, 1971.

10. Anthology or Compilation
Lawall, Sarah N., and Maynard Mack, eds. <u>The Norton Anthology of World Masterpieces</u>. 2nd ed. Expanded ed. New York: Norton, 2001.

11. Selection from an Anthology
Thoreau, Henry David. "Civil Disobedience." <u>Literature and Society</u>. Ed. Pamela J. Annas and Robert C. Rosen. 3rd ed. Upper Saddle River, NJ: Prentice Hall, 2001. 1331–1346.

12. Reference Work: Encyclopedia or Dictionary
"Cloning." <u>Grolier Encyclopedia of Knowledge</u>. 1991 ed.

"United States Population." <u>The World Almanac and Book of Facts</u>. 2001.

13. Multivolume Work
Wilkie, Brian, and James Hurt, eds. <u>Literature of the Western World</u>. 5th ed. 2 vols. Upper Saddle River, NJ: Prentice Hall, 2001.

14. Book in a Series
Martini, Alberto. <u>Renoir</u>. The Avenel Art Library. 3. New York: Avenel Books, 1978.

15. Bible
<u>The NIV Study Bible</u>. Kenneth Barker, gen. ed. Grand Rapids, MI: Zondervan, 1995.

16. Introduction, Preface, Forward, or Afterword
Bellow, Saul. Forward. <u>The Closing of the American Mind</u>. By Allan Bloom. New York: Simon & Schuster, 1987. 11–18.

Periodicals
Author's last name, first name. "Article Title," <u>Periodical Title</u> Date: Page number(s).

17. Article in a Weekly
Begley, Sharon. "Science Finds God." <u>Newsweek</u> 20 July 1998: 46–51.

18. Article in a Monthly
Wilkinson, Todd. "The Cultural Challenge." <u>National Parks</u> Jan.–Feb. 2000: 20–23.

19. Article in a Newspaper
Russell, Sabin. "Federal Panel Urges Tests of Medical Pot." <u>San Francisco Chronicle</u> 18 Mar. 1999: A1.

20. Article in a Journal Paginated by Issue
Clarke, Arthur. "Beyond Gravity." <u>National Geographic</u> 199.1 (2001): 2–5.

21. Article in a Journal Paginated by Volume (Yearly)
Annas, George J. "Reefer Madness—The Federal Response to California's Medical Marijuana Law." <u>New England Journal of Medicine</u> 337 (1997): 435–439.

22. Editorial
McCormick, Steven J. "Confronting a Change in Climate." Editorial. <u>Nature Conservancy</u> Sep.–Oct. 2001: 5.

23. Unsigned Article
"Computing in Comfort." <u>Consumer Reports</u> Sep. 2001: 20–24.

24. Letter to the Editor
Stanley, Julian C. Letter. <u>American Educator</u> 24.1 (2000): 2.

Arce, Larry J. Letter. <u>The Fresno Bee</u> 2 Sep. 2001: G2.

25. Review
Ansen, David. "Playing to the Crowds." Rev. of <u>The Mask of Zorro</u>, dir. Martin Campbell. <u>Newsweek</u> 20 July 1998: 66.

26. A Special Issue

Scientists & Thinkers of the 20th Century. Spec. issue of Time 153.12 (1999): 1–232.

Other Sources (nonelectronic)

27. Government Publication

California Department of Fish and Game. Sport Fishing Regulations. Sacramento, State of California, 2000.

28. Pamphlet

Boy Scouts of America. How to Protect Your Children from Child Abuse and Drug Abuse: A Parent's Guide. Irving, TX: BSA, 1991.

29. Published Interview

Belafonte, Harry. Interview with James Brady. Parade 16 Sep. 2001: 22.

30. Personal Interview

Weston, William. Personal interview. 15 Nov. 1999.

31. Radio or Television Program

Jazz. Dir. Ken Burns. Narr. Keith David. PBS. WETA, Washington. Jan. 2001.

32. Radio or Television Interview

Powell, Colin. Interview with Peter Jennings. Nightline. ABC. WABC, New York. 1 Aug. 2000.

33. Film or Video

Schindler's List. Dir. Steven Spielberg. Perf. Liam Neeson and Ralph Fiennes. Universal, 1993.

34. Live Performance (Play, Opera, Ballet, Concert)

A Streetcar Named Desire. By Tennessee Williams. Dir. Elia Kazan. Perf. Marlon Brando, Kim Hunter, Karl Malden, and Jessica Tandy. Barrymore Theatre, New York. 3 Dec. 1947.

35. Musical Composition

Beethoven, Ludwig van. Concerto no. 2 in B.

36. Personal Letter or Memo

Bradbury, Ray. Letter to author. 21 May 1977.

37. Published Letter

Twain, Mark. "To William Dean Howells." 23 Nov. 1877. Letter. The Portable Mark Twain. Ed. Bernard DeVoto. New York, Viking, 1967.

38. Lecture or Personal Address (Speech, Sermon, Reading)

King, Jr., Martin Luther. "I Have a Dream." National Mall, Washington, DC. 28 Aug. 1963.

39. Published Dissertation

Lehner, Luis. Gravitational Radiation from Black Hole Spacetimes. Diss. U of Pittsburgh, 1998. Ann Arbor: UMI, 1998.

40. Unpublished Dissertation

Nicholson, Maxwell. "The Hemingway Hero: WWI vs. WWII." Diss. U. of Michigan, 1995.

41. Dissertation Abstract

Andrews, Kenneth T. "'Freedom Is a Constant Struggle': The Dynamics and Consequences of the Mississippi Civil Rights Movement, 1960–1984." Diss. SUNY at Stony Brook, 1997. DAI-A 59 (1998): 620A.

42. Proceedings of a Conference

Hagen, C. R., ed. Theoretical High Energy Physics: MRST 2000. AIP Conference Proceedings, May 8–9, 2000, Rochester, NY. Melville, NY: AIP Press, 2000.

43. Sound Recording

Davis, Miles. Kind of Blue. Columbia, 1997.

44. An Advertisement

Jergens Skin Care. Advertisement. Prevention Sep. 2001: 32–33.

45. Legal Source

Miller v. California. 413 U.S. 15. 1973.

US Const. Art. 3, sec. 2.

46. Work of Art

Van Gogh, Vincent. Portrait of Dr. Gachet. 1890. Musée du Louvre, Paris.

47. Cartoon

Adams, Scott. "Dilbert." Cartoon. The Fresno Bee 1 Sep. 2001: E8.

48. Map or Chart

Canada. Map. Chicago: Rand, 2001.

Electronic Sources

49. Online Scholarly Project or Information Database

The Electronic Text Center. Ed. David Seaman. 2000. Alderman Lib., U of Virginia. 2 June 2000 <http://etext.lib.virginia.edu/>.

50. Document in an Online Scholarly Project or Information Database

"This Day in History: September 11." The History Channel Online. 2001. History Channel. 17 Sep. 2001 <http://www.historychannel.com/>.

51. Personal or Professional Website

King, Stephen. Home page. 31 Aug. 2001 <http://www.horrorking.com/>.

52. Online Book or Text

Whitman, Walt. Leaves of Grass. Brooklyn, 1855. 19 Apr. 2001 <http://jefferson. village.virginia.edu/Whitman/works/leaves/1855/text.frameset.html>.

53. Article in an Online Periodical (magazine or journal)

Horowitz, David. "By Any Means." Salon 22 Nov. 2000. 30 Jan. 2001 <http://www.salon.com/news/col/horo/2000/11/22/gore/index.html>.

54. Article in an Online Periodical (newspaper or newswire)

Gosselin, Peter G., and Warren Vieth. "Washington Acts to Head Off Financial Downturn." Los Angeles Times 17 Sep. 2001. 17 Sep. 2001 <http://www.latimes.com/business/ as-091701econ.story>.

55. Publication on a CD-ROM, Diskette, or Magnetic Tape

"Lightning." Compton's Interactive Encyclopedia, 1995 Edition. CD-ROM. Cambridge, MA: Softkey, 1995.

56. E-mail Communication

Bruque, George. "Re: City Arts artwork." E-mail to the author. 18 Sep. 2001.

57. Online Posting

Arafin, Shameel. "Beyond Magic." Online posting. 9 Aug. 1995. The RoundTable Forum: HyperNews. 20 Sep. 1999 <http://hypernews.org>.

58. Work from an Online Subscription Service

Grier, Peter. "A Changed World, Part 1: The Attack." The Christian Science Monitor 17 Sep. 2001: Proquest Direct. Fresno City College Lib., FCC, Fresno, CA. 18 Sep. 2001 <http://proquest.umi.com/pqdweb>.

59. Synchronous Communication

McDonald, Lucy Tribble. TCC-L 1998 Online Conference. 8 Apr. 1998. DaMOO. 23 Feb. 2000 <http://damoo.csun.edu:8888/>.

60. Other Online Sources

"Pismo Beach, CA, US." Map. MapQuest. 2001. 1 Aug. 2001 <http://www.mapquest.com/ cgi-bin/>.

CHAPTER 25

APA Documentation Style

1. In-Text Citations	2. Reference List
	2.1 Guidelines for APA Reference List
	2.2 Basic Elements for APA Reference Lists

As mentioned previously, when using information gathered from research, you *must* document your sources. Whether the information you use is quoted, paraphrased, or summarized, if it is not common knowledge, then you must cite your sources. The basic documentation style of the American Psychological Association (APA) is shown below. For more detailed information on APA style, consult the *Publication Manual of the American Psychological Association* (5th ed., 2001) or the APA Web site (http://www.apastyle.org).

1. IN-TEXT CITATIONS

The APA uses in-text citations rather than footnotes or endnotes to cite sources. The citation requires at least two pieces of information: (1) the author's last name, and (2) the year of publication. If the information is quoted directly, then the page number(s) of where the information was found is also required (preceded by "p." or "pp."). The author(s) may be mentioned in the text material along with the information or named after the information is given (last name only) inside parentheses with the publication date and page number(s).

EXAMPLES: IN-TEXT CITATIONS

Name(s) mentioned in text material; page number(s) at the end

According to researchers Michael Grubb and Niels Meyer (1993), "migrating waterfowl . . . often change course at a great distance from wind turbines, and species that once fed in the vicinity of a windfarm apparently adapt rapidly to the presence of wind turbines and learn to avoid the rotors" (p. 173).

Chiles (2000) reported that the electrical output of one nuclear power plant is about 1,000 megawatts.

Name(s) given after the information; page number(s) at end

"Migrating waterfowl . . . often change course at a great distance from wind turbines, and species that once fed in the vicinity of a windfarm apparently adapt rapidly to the presence of wind turbines and learn to avoid the rotors" (Grubb & Meyer, 1993, p. 173).

The electrical output of one nuclear power plant is about 1,000 megawatts (Chiles, 2000).

---

2. REFERENCE LIST

At the end of your paper, the sources of information that you used are listed with complete publication information. This list in APA style is called **References**. It lists your sources, *alphabetically,* by author's (or editor's) last name (or, if no author, by first word in the article title, but not *a, an,* or *the*). List only the sources you actually used and cited in your paper, not everything you researched and read (unless your instructor requires you to list all sources consulted).

EXAMPLE: REFERENCE LIST

References listing for in-text citations (p. 89):

> Chiles, J. (2000, March). A second wind. *Smithsonian, 30,* 54–58.
> Grubb, M. J., & Meyer, N. I. (1993). Wind energy: Resources, systems, and regional strategies. In Thomas B. Johansson, et al. (Eds.), *Renewable energy: Sources for fuels and electricity* (pp. 167–189). Washington, DC: Island.

2.1 Guidelines for APA References List

- The References list should begin on a separate page at the end of the paper.
- The word References should be centered five spaces below the short title and page number at the top of the page.
- Do not put the word References in quotation marks or italics, or spell it with all capital letters.
- List references alphabetically, not in the order you cited them in the paper.
- Begin every listing at the left-hand margin. If the information runs more than one line, indent each line after the first.
- Double-space the listings throughout the list.
- Do not number the listings.

Basic formats for the most common References listings follow the directory, Figure 25.1.

Figure 25.1 APA Reference Listings Directory

Directory for APA Reference list

Periodicals
1. Basic Elements for a Journal Article, Paginated by Volume
2. Article in a Journal Paginated by Issue
3. Article in a Magazine
4. Signed Article in a Daily Newspaper
5. Unsigned Article in a Daily Newspaper
6. Abstract as an Original Source
7. Letter to the Editor in Weekly Newspaper Article

Books
8. Basic Elements for an Entire Book
9. Edition Other Than First
10. Multiple Authors
11. Group or Corporate Author
12. Editor(s) or Edited Book
13. No Author or Editor
14. Encyclopedia or Dictionary
15. English Translation of a Book

(continued)

16. Brochure: Group or Corporate Author or Organization
17. Article or Chapter in an Edited Book

Other

18. Personal Communications (E-mail, personal interviews, etc.)

Technical and Research Reports

19. Basic Elements of a Government or Document Deposit Service Report
20. Report from a Private Organization

Proceedings of Meetings and Symposia

21. Published Proceedings of a Conference or Symposium
22. Proceedings Published Regularly

Doctoral Dissertations

23. Doctoral Dissertation
24. Unpublished Doctoral Dissertation

Audiovisual Media

25. Motion Picture
26. Television Broadcast
27. Television Series
28. Music Recording

Electronic Media

29. Internet Article from a Print Source
30. Article in an Internet-only Journal
31. Journal Article from a Database
32. Newspaper Article, Electronic Version
33. Paper Presented at a Virtual Conference
34. Message Posted to an Online Forum or Discussion Group

2.2   Basic Elements for APA Reference Lists

Periodicals

1. Basic Elements for a Journal Article, Paginated by Volume

Author's last name, Initials. (Date of publication). Article title. *Periodical Title, Volume number,* Page
     number(s).

(**Note:** All other listings for periodicals are variations of this basic format.)

Brass, E. P. (2001). Changing the status of drugs from prescription to over-the-counter availability.
     New England Journal of Medicine, 345, 810–814.

2. Article in a Journal Paginated by Issue

Clarke, A. (2001). Beyond gravity. *National Geographic, 199*(1), 2–5.

3. Article in a Magazine

Begley, S. (1998, July 20). Science finds God. *Newsweek,* 46–51.

4. Signed Article in a Daily Newspaper

Russell, S. (1999, March 18). Federal panel urges tests of medical pot. *San Francisco Chronicle,* p. A1.

5. Unsigned Article in a Daily Newspaper

Male hypertension linked to genetics. (2001, September 24). *USA Today,* p. 6D.

6. Abstract as an Original Source

Gahan, L. J., Gould, F., & Heckel, D. G. (2001, August 3). Identification of a gene associated with Bt resistance in *Heliothis virescens* [Abstract]. *Science, 293,* 857.

7. Letter to the Editor in Weekly Newspaper Article

Miller, H. I. (2001, September 20). Biological warfare: The 'good' news. *The Wall Street Journal,* p. A17.

Books

8. Basic Elements for an Entire Book

Author's last name, Initials. (Year). *Book title.* City of Publication: Publisher.
(*Note:* All other listings for books are variations of this basic format.)
Hawking, S. (1988). *A brief history of time.* New York: Bantam.

9. Edition Other Than First

Rosenberg, D. (1999). *World mythology* (3rd ed.). Lincolnwood, IL: NTC/Contemporary.

10. Multiple Authors (two to six authors, list all; if more than six authors, list first six, then add et al.)

McDonald, D., & Burton, L. W. (2002). *The language of argument* (10th ed.). New York: Longman.

11. Group or Corporate Author (If the group or corporation is the publisher, also put "Author.")

American Psychological Association. (2001). *Publication Manual of the American Psychological Association* (5th ed.). Washington, DC: Author.

12. Editor(s) or Edited Book

Bennett, W. J. (Ed.). (1995). *The moral compass.* New York: Simon & Schuster.

13. No Author or Editor

Grolier new Webster's dictionary. (1992). Danbury, CT: Grolier.

14. Encyclopedia or Dictionary

Lorimer, L. T., et al. (Eds.). (1991). *Grolier encyclopedia of knowledge.* (Vols. 1–20). Danbury, CT: Grolier.

15. English Translation of a Book

Marquez, G. G. (1971). *One hundred years of solitude.* (G. Rabassa, Trans.) New York: Bard-Avon. (Original work published 1967)

16. Brochure: Group or Corporate Author or Organization

Bank of America. (2000). *Facts about personal deposit account programs.* [Brochure]. San Francisco: Author.

17. Article or Chapter in an Edited Book

Thoreau, H. D. (2001). Civil disobedience. In P. J. Annas & R. C. Rosen (Eds.), *Literature and society* (3rd ed.) (pp. 1331–1346). Upper Saddle River, NJ: Prentice Hall.

Other

18. Personal Communications (E-mail, personal interviews, telephone interviews, letters, memos, electronic bulletin boards, nonarchived discussion groups, etc.)
These communications should be cited in the text of your document, but because they are not "recoverable" or available to others, APA does not list them in the References listing.

Example: R. P. Chenn (personal communication, December 14, 2000).

Technical and Research Reports

19. Basic Elements of a Government or Document Deposit Service Report

Author or Government Institute. (Year of Publication). Report title (Report or Publication number, if given). City of Publication: Publisher (Document Deposit Service number, if from a depository).
U.S. Department of Justice. (1999). *Crime in the United States, 1999, uniform crime reports* (ISBN 0-16-050489-9). Washington, DC: U.S. Government Printing Office.

20. Report From a Private Organization

Council for American Families. (2000, November). *American families in crisis, 1975–2000*
(Publication No. 00103). St. Louis: Author.

Proceedings of Meetings and Symposia

21. Published Proceedings of a Conference or Symposium

Appiah, A. K. (1998). The limits of pluralism. In Melzer, A. M., Weinberger, J., & Zinman, M. R.
(Eds.), *Symposium on Science, Reason, and Modern Democracy. Multiculturalism and American
democracy* (pp. 37–54). Lawrence: University Press of Kansas.

22. Proceedings Published Regularly

Gambetta, G. A., & Lagarias, J. C. (2001). Genetic engineering of phytochrome biosynthesis in
bacteria. *Proceedings of the National Academy of Sciences, USA, 98,* 10566–10571.

Doctoral Dissertations

23. Doctoral Dissertation

Andrews, K. T. (1998). 'Freedom is a constant struggle': The dynamics and consequences of the
Mississippi civil rights movement, 1960–1984. *Dissertation Abstracts International, 59*(02),
620A. (UMI No. 9824679)

24. Unpublished Doctoral Dissertation

Nichols, I. M. (1999). *Interpersonal relationship analysis of fraternal twins.* Unpublished doctoral
dissertation. University of Illinois, Urbana.

Audiovisual Media

25. Motion Picture

Spielberg, S. (Director). (1993). *Schindler's list* [Motion picture]. United States: Universal.

26. Television Broadcast

Koppel, T. (Host). (2001, September 11). *Nightline* [Television broadcast]. New York: American
Broadcasting Company.

27. Television Series

Burns, K. (Director). (2001). *Jazz* [Television series]. Washington, DC: WETA.

28. Music Recording

Davis, M. (1997). All blues. On *Kind of blue* [CD]. New York: Columbia.

Electronic Media

29. Internet Article From a Print Source

Root, G. P. M. (2001). Sanitation, community environments, and childhood diarrhoea in rural
Zimbabwe [Electronic version]. *Journal of Health, Population, and Nutrition, 19,* 73–82.

30. Article in an Internet-only Journal

Horowitz, D. (2000, November 22). By any means. *Salon.* Retrieved January 30, 2001, from
http://www.salon.com/news/col/horo/2000/11/22/gore/ index.html.

31. Journal Article from a Database

Devereux, P. G., & Ginsburg, G. P. (2001). Sociality effects on the production of laughter. *Journal of
General Psychology, 128,* 227–241. Retrieved September 26, 2001, from ProQuest database.

32. Newspaper Article, Electronic Version

Gosselin, P. G., & Vieth, W. (2001, September 17) Washington acts to head off financial downturn.
Los Angeles Times. Retrieved September 17, 2001, from http://www.latimes.com/business/
as-091701econ.story.

33. Paper Presented at a Virtual Conference

McDonald, L. T. (1998). *Creation myths of cyberspace.* Paper presented at the TCC-L 1998 Online
Conference. Retrieved February 23, 2000, from http://damoo.csun.edu:8888/.

34. Message Posted to an Online Forum or Discussion Group

Arafin, S. (1995, August 9). Beyond magic [Msg 2]. Message posted to The RoundTable Forum:
HyperNews, archived at http://hypernews.org.

CHAPTER 26
Goal Setting

1. Setting Goals

1. SETTING GOALS

Many students say that the reason they are going to college is to get a good job and make a lot of money. But how will they do this? What is that "good" job? How much money is "a lot"? Finding answers to these questions is not easy. You need to have a good understanding of who you are, what your likes and dislikes are as well as your strengths and weaknesses. As you begin to make decisions about what you want to do in your life, it is time to set goals. Setting goals helps you to focus on your direction. Goals are maps that help you get to where you want to go. Goals can be either short term or long term depending on what you are trying to achieve. Follow these suggestions when setting goals:

- *Set goals that truly express what you want, not just those that sound good.* For example, don't say you want to make a lot of money when you finish college. Instead say that you want your first job after college to pay at least thirty thousand dollars from the start.
- *Make your goals realistic.* For example, you might want to get 100 percent on every test you take. However, is it possible to be perfect every time?
- *Write down your goals and the steps necessary to meet them.* One goal may be to become a doctor. By writing down the steps necessary to become one, you may discover that you may or may not want to devote the amount of time and work required to become one.
- *Write positive goals, not negative ones.* Don't write a goal which states that you don't want a dead-end job. This does not help you focus on what you *do* want. Write what you want. For example, say, "I want to be a computer programmer for a corporation."
- *Set a reasonable time frame.* By setting a beginning and completion date, you will be better able to stay on track. However, make your time frame for achieving your goal realistic, so you won't become too discouraged or abandon your plans altogether.
- *Allow room for flexibility.* There will always be setbacks that you cannot anticipate or changes that you want to make. Set your goals with enough flexibility to accommodate those setbacks or changes.
- *Set priorities.* Most people have more than one goal at a time. Decide which ones are most important to work on so that you don't become overloaded and unable to achieve any of them.
- *Set goals that can be measured.* If your goal is to have a good job and make enough money to be comfortable in life, you'll find it difficult to know what a good job is, how much money is enough, and what it means to be happy without any means of measuring your success.

Goal setting takes effort, and reaching goals takes time, preparation, and patience. However, as the old saying goes, you can't reach your goals if you don't set any goals. Set your goals wisely and work diligently to reach them.

Exercise 26.1

Directions: Use the guide below to help you set your short-term and long-term goals.

Semester Goals

1. What are three goals I wish to meet by the end of this semester? (Write them in order of importance.)

   1. _____
   2. _____
   3. _____

2. How will I meet each goal?

   1. _____
   2. _____
   3. _____

3. How will I measure these goals?

   1. _____
   2. _____
   3. _____

One-Year Goals

1. What are three goals I wish to meet by the end of this year? (Write them in order of importance.)

   1. _____
   2. _____
   3. _____

2. How will I meet each goal?

   1. _____
   2. _____
   3. _____

3. How will I measure these goals?

   1. _____
   2. _____
   3. _____

Five-Year Goals

1. What are three goals I wish to meet by the end of five years? (Write them in order of importance.)

   1. _____
   2. _____
   3. _____

2. How will I meet each goal?

    1. _____

    2. _____

    3. _____

3. How will I measure these goals?

    1. _____

    2. _____

    3. _____

Ten-Year Goals

1. What are three goals I wish to meet by the end of ten years (Write them in order of importance.)

    1. _____

    2. _____

    3. _____

2. How will I meet each goal?

    1. _____

    2. _____

    3. _____

3. How will I measure these goals?

    1. _____

    2. _____

    3. _____

Discussion Topic

Form groups of three or four members. Share with each member of the group what your goals are and how you will meet them.

Note: It would be interesting to keep a copy of your goals and look at them ten years from now to see what you achieved. There are bound to be some surprises.

CHAPTER 27

Time Management

1. Analyze Your Time Commitments	3. Develop a Study Plan
2. Develop a Weekly Schedule	

10/14/12

One of the basic reasons why some students fail to do well in school is because they don't manage their time well. Some students put off doing their homework, writing papers, and studying for tests until the last minute. Others schedule so many activities into the day that they cannot spend enough time on assignments to do a thorough job. Managing your time properly is not only an important skill for school, but also one you will need in your career. Follow the steps below to become more efficient with your time management.

1. ANALYZE YOUR TIME COMMITMENTS

The first step is to analyze what you are doing with your time. By doing this, you can see at a glance how much time is taken up with school, work, and other commitments. Estimate how many hours you spend each week committed to the activities below.

Activities	Hours
Classes	5
Studying	~~8~~ 14
Meals	7
Work	~~24~~ hrs 40
Transportation/Commuting	4.5
Grooming	(sleep – 7·7) 49 + 7 = 56
Other activities (sports, hobbies)	~~8~~ 30
Total	~~145~~ = ~~116~~ 156.50

Subtract your total from 168, the number of hours in a week. The remainder is the amount of uncommitted time you have. ~~145~~ 156.5 =

168 − ~~145~~ = ~~23.50~~ ⟨~~20~~ 11.5⟩

If you have little or no uncommitted time, then you are overextended and need to reevaluate your commitments.

2. DEVELOP A WEEKLY SCHEDULE

Now that you have an idea how your time is being used, the next step is to develop a weekly schedule (see Figure 27.1, p. 98, and do Exercise 27.2, p. 100). This schedule will help you keep on track in completing your assignments and other commitments. Include in this schedule the times you have class, go to work, study, and any other commitments. Try to be realistic in how much you can accomplish in one day. Also make your schedule as flexible as possible. You don't want one unforeseen emergency to throw your schedule into chaos. When figuring the amount of time you need for studying, use the 2-for-1 method. Most colleges use the formula that for every one hour of class, you should be studying or doing homework for two hours. Thus, if you are in class for 12 hours per week, you should be studying for 24 hours outside of class.

Figure 27.1 Sample Weekly Schedule

	Monday	Tuesday	Wednesday	Thursday	Friday	Saturday	Sunday
7:00 AM	Wake up	Wake up	Wake up	Wake up	Wake up		
8:00 AM	English 1A		English 1A		English 1A		
9:00 AM		Volleyball		Volleyball			
10:00 AM	Spanish 3	Spanish 3 Lab	Spanish 3		Spanish 3		
11:00 AM	Study	Lunch	Study	Lunch	Study		
12:00 PM	Lunch	Study	Lunch	Study	Lunch		
1:00 PM	Study	History 12	Study	History 12	Study	Study	
2:00 PM	Math 5		Math 5		Math 5		Study
3:00 PM		Library Study			Library Study		
4:00 PM							
5:00 PM							
6:00 PM			Work	Work			
7:00 PM	Work					Work	
8:00 PM		Study			Study		
9:00 PM							
10:00 PM							
11:00 PM							

3. DEVELOP A STUDY PLAN

Now that you have a weekly schedule, the next step is to develop a study plan. Although you have blocked out time for study, you must make efficient use of that time. You don't want your time eaten away by distractions. Follow these suggestions in developing your plan.

- *Find a quiet place to study.* This could be the library, your bedroom, or any quiet place where you can concentrate.

- *Turn off your pager and let your answering machine screen your calls.* Talking on the telephone will eat away your time quickly.

- *Have all of the equipment you need to study.* This includes pens, pencils, paper, calculators, and anything else that is required to do your work.

- *Study your difficult subjects first.* You want to study these subjects when your mind is fresh and alert.

- *Study a subject the day before the class meets.* This will help to reinforce your learning and prepare you for class.

- *Take short breaks.* If you are studying for a long time, a ten-minute break is needed every hour to help your mind refocus. You should also take a short break when changing subjects.

- *Break down big assignments into manageable chunks.* If you know what you can do in the time you have set aside, you will not feel so overwhelmed.

- *Write questions and notes about what you are studying.* With these notes, you can look for further information or ask your teacher or classmates for clarification.

Following and practicing these techniques will help you to manage your time and to study more effectively and efficiently. As you become better at these techniques, studying will become more natural to you and your grades will improve.

Exercise 27.1

Directions: Develop your own study plan by answering the prompts below.

1. Where is a quiet place that I can study? _room with door Shut_

2. What types of things distract me from studying? _tv, Chores around house, kids activities, noise_

3. What can I do to stop these distractions from occurring? _Study outside of home_

4. What type of equipment do I need for my studies? _Computer, notebook, pen, books_

5. What times will I be able to study? _evenings_

6. In what order will I study for my classes? _?_

7. How long can I study before I need a break to refocus? _2 hrs_

Exercise 27.2

Directions: Develop your weekly schedule (see Figure 27.1).

	Monday	Tuesday	Wednesday	Thursday	Friday	Saturday	Sunday
7:00 AM	Wake-up						
8:00 AM			work				
9:00 AM	Work	work		work	work		
10:00 AM							
11:00 AM							
12:00 PM			Rotary				
1:00 PM	Lunch	Lunch		Lunch	Lunch		
2:00 PM							Study
3:00 PM							
4:00 PM							
5:00 PM	End Work						
6:00 PM	School	School					
7:00 PM			Homework			Study	
8:00 PM							
9:00 PM							
10:00 PM	Downtime						
11:00 PM	Sleep						

CHAPTER 28

Resource Management

> ## 1. Basic Resources and Services at College

Colleges provide a wide variety of services to help you achieve your goals and get the most out of your college experience. It is important to check your college catalog to see what is offered at your college. The following is a list of the basic services found at most colleges.

1. BASIC RESOURCES AND SERVICES AT COLLEGE

- *Academic Counseling Center* helps students plan their programs.
- *Career Center* helps students plan a college major or career direction.
- *Computer labs* provide computers for students to access programs that enhance their studies and allow word processing, Internet access, and so on.
- *Disability services* provide assistance for students with physical and learning disabilities.
- *Financial Aid Office* provides financial assistance in the form of grants, loans, scholarships, and/or employment.
- *Health services* provide different levels of health care.
- *Libraries* offer an abundance of materials and tools to support students' studies.
- *Psychological services* help students in need of psychological health care.
- *Student activities and clubs* may include intramural sports, student government, and special interest clubs.
- *Student learning center* allows students to volunteer time in companies that may be of interest in their major field of study.
- *Study abroad programs* allow students to attend schools in different countries.
- *Tutorial center* provides free tutoring services.

These services and others are located on most campuses and are available to all students. They exist to serve and help students, so take advantage of what they have to offer. They can help make your college experience better and more enjoyable.

Discussions

1. In groups, discuss what resources are available at your school and where they are located. Share your information with the other groups in your class.
2. In groups, discuss which resources you have used at your school. Explain whether or not these resources were helpful and why. Share your information with the other groups in your class.

CHAPTER 29

Diversity on Campus

1. Types of Diversity
   - 1.1 Racial
   - 1.2 Ethnic
   - 1.3 Cultural
   - 1.4 Sexual
   - 1.5 Religious
   - 1.6 Age

Because of the changing demographics in the United States and its more inclusive educational system, the diversity of the U.S. student population has made life on college campuses more exciting and interesting. Now more than ever before, you have a tremendous opportunity to experience different cultures, beliefs, and world views. Learning about and experiencing the wide range of diversity found at your college will not only help you understand those with differing backgrounds, but can help you gain a better understanding of yourself. Socializing with people from diverse backgrounds will help you broaden your horizons and appreciate different viewpoints. Look for opportunities to meet people from diverse backgrounds by getting involved in sports and club activities and attending cultural celebrations on campus. During class, share your experiences when relevant and listen attentively to others when they share theirs. Almost all colleges offer courses in various cultural studies. Enroll in one or two of these classes. Involving yourself in diversity enriches your life and the lives of those around you.

1. TYPES OF DIVERSITY

1.1 Racial

Race is what most people think of first when diversity is mentioned because it is so easily observed. The United States of America is probably the most racially mixed country in the world because of its traditional open-door policy for immigration. However, there are still places in America that lack racial diversity. Therefore, for some students college may be the first opportunity to associate and make friends with people from different racial backgrounds. You will learn that outward appearance is only a superficial difference between people.

1.2 Ethnic

Many countries have a more restricted immigration policy than the United States. However, this does not mean that other countries have only one ethnic group living there. If you were to meet three people from the country of Ethiopia, the chances are that one may be Amhara, one Tigrean, and the other Oromo. Each is a different ethnic group that speaks a different language and follows different customs. At your college, you may have the opportunity to learn from the students you meet from all over the world about the diversity that can be found in any country.

1.3 Cultural

Cultural diversity can be found not only by meeting people from other countries but also within your own country. If you are from the West Coast and move to the East Coast, you will encounter some different points of view. Moving from the South to the Pacific Northwest would expose you to a whole new set of customs and attitudes. In most colleges, it is possible to meet and learn about people from all over America.

1.4 Sexual

The last three decades have seen an increase in the openness and acceptance of people with different sexual orientations. As with any other type of diversity discussed in this section, once this superficial difference is removed, you will discover that we all share similar goals, hopes, and dreams.

1.5 Religious

Some consider America to be predominantly a Christian country, but if you stop to think about what that means, you will realize that there are many different groups of Christians that hold different opinions about their beliefs and how to follow them. Moreover, again because of immigration, other religions can also be found here. You will discover that there are many different religious organizations on the college campus and, therefore, you have the opportunity to learn about the different religious beliefs.

1.6 Age

You have probably noticed while walking through campus or sitting in class that there are students of all ages on campus. One of the strengths of American higher education is the fact that people of any age can enroll and work toward receiving a college degree or credit. Older students bring many qualities to a class, such as experience with work, families, and unique life experiences, all of which can enrich everyone's learning experience.

Discussions

1. In this chapter, six types of diversity were mentioned. In groups, identify and discuss other types of diversity that can found on a college campus. Share your answers with the other groups.
2. Look at your college catalog to find the different types of organizations that exist on your campus. Which ones would you like to join and why?

CHAPTER 30

College and Disabilities

1. People and Disabilities
2. Disability Services and Programs
   2.1 Disabilities Office or Program
   2.2 Services Offered
   2.3 Visit the Disabilities Office
3. Accommodations and Arrangements
   3.1 Services and Programs
   3.2 Instructors
   3.3 Other Students

1. PEOPLE AND DISABILITIES

Disability can be a difficult topic to talk about.If you have ever suffered a disability or known someone who has, you may have some understanding of the difficulties involved. A disability can make life very challenging.

We should be mindful of how we look at others and avoid making assumptions. Some disabilities are obvious and some are not. Of course, it's rather obvious if someone is in a wheelchair or blind, but not all disabilities are outwardly visible. Some people suffer chronic or painful ailments; others struggle with learning disabilities, which cannot be seen. The important thing is to look beyond the disability and see the person.

It may help to remember that disabilities are often caused by tragic misfortunes in life and it takes substantial courage to overcome such obstacles and get on with living. In such circumstances, taking on the additional challenges of college often requires great strength of character.

2. DISABILITY SERVICES AND PROGRAMS

Colleges and universities have increasingly been eliminating the barriers to students with learning or physical disabilities. Most campuses have services and programs to assist disabled students in pursuing their college career. If you need such services or suspect that you might, you should familiarize yourself with what services are available on your campus.

2.1 Office or Program

First, check to see if your campus has a special office or program for disabled students. Also check to see if counselors are available who specialize in assisting disabled students.

2.2 Services Offered

Second, find out what services are offered for disabled students. On most campuses, services range from college career planning to priority registration to special parking permits, plus numerous other support services.

2.3 Visit the Disabilities Office

Third, make an appointment to visit the office on campus and pick up some program information or talk with a counselor.

3. ACCOMMODATIONS AND ARRANGEMENTS

Depending on the disability, most colleges also offer various accommodations to help students succeed with their classes. In the classroom, arrangements can be made for note-takers or interpreters for hearing-impaired students. Special seating can be arranged for those with physical handicaps. Sometimes students may be allowed some help or leeway with certain assignments if their disability would put them at a disadvantage. Students with physical or learning disabilities may also receive some accommodation when taking tests. In some colleges, the administration allows accommodations ranging from assistance with class schedules, to providing elevator keys, to special consideration of degree requirements. These and many more services are available at most campuses for those who need them.

3.1 Services and Programs

Take advantage of the services and programs at your campus. They are there to assist you.

3.2 Instructors

Get to know your instructors. At least introduce yourself and ask to speak with them if you think you want or need some accommodation with the class, for example, seating, test taking, requesting a note-taker, or whatever. Most college instructors will be pleased to listen and to help you. If you are too nervous or too shy to ask, then go through your counselor or the disabled students program.

3.3 Other Students

Make contact with other students in your classes. (This is a good idea for all students to do.) It's always handy to know someone in each class with whom you can study or share notes on days when one of you misses class. Most people are friendly if given a chance. Be bold—introduce yourself.

A disability can be limiting enough as it is. Don't limit yourself further by trying to go it alone. Take full advantage of the services and programs available on your campus. They are there to benefit all who need them.

Exercises

1. As a class or in groups, have an open and frank discussion about disabilities. Take particular notice of those disabilities you have never heard of before. Consider what the challenges of living with certain disabilities might be and how you would handle them.
2. Write a short paper on the challenges of a particular disability and how you think you would handle them. If you are a student with a disability, write about the challenges you face and how you handle them.
3. Locate the Disability Services Office on your campus and find out what kind of services and programs are available. Collect brochures or make a list. Also find out what opportunities exist for students to help others with disabilities and make a list. For example, most campuses will enlist or hire students to be note-takers or readers or allow them to proctor exams taken in the office.

CHAPTER 31

The Basics of the Parts of Speech

1. Nouns
   1.1 Proper Nouns and Common Nouns
   1.2 Countable Nouns
   1.3 Uncountable Nouns
2. Pronouns
3. Verbs
   3.1 Types of Verbs
       3.1.1 Action Verbs
       3.1.2 Transitive Verbs
       3.1.3 Intransitive Verbs
       3.1.4 Linking Verbs
       3.1.5 Auxiliary Verbs

4. Adjectives
5. Adverbs
6. Articles
7. Prepositions
8. Conjunctions

1. NOUNS

A noun refers to a person, place, or thing. Nouns are used as either the subject or the object of a sentence. If the noun is the *subject,* it is performing an action or is being described. To find the subject of the sentence, ask yourself who or what is doing something, or who or what is being described in the sentence.

> *Examples:* a. *Sociologists* study society.
> b. *Linguistics* is the study of language.

In example (a), sociologists perform the action of studying. In example (b), linguistics is being described as the study of language.

If a noun is the *object* of the sentence, it is receiving the action of the verb.

> *Examples:* a. Debbie ate a large *hamburger.*
> b. Patti plays the *banjo.*

In example (a), the *hamburger* is receiving the action of being eaten. In example (b), the *banjo* is receiving the action of being played.

1.1 Proper Nouns and Common Nouns

There are two types of nouns: proper and common. A *proper* noun is a word that names a particular person, place, or thing. It is capitalized in the middle of the sentence. A *common* noun is the general name of a person, place, or thing and is not capitalized in the middle of a sentence.

> *Example: Lee* went to *China* for his *vacation.*

Lee and *China* are proper nouns because they are the particular names of a person and place, whereas *vacation* is a common noun.

1.2 Countable Nouns

Nouns are either singular (one) or plural (two or more). If a noun can be made plural, it is called a *countable* noun. To make a noun plural add either -*s* or -*es* to the end of the word.

1.3 Uncountable Nouns

Uncountable nouns represent things or concepts that cannot be counted. These nouns are either *abstract*, *concrete*, or *collective* nouns.

> *Example:* America won its *independence* from England.

Independence represents a concept that cannot be made plural. Words like this are called *abstract nouns*. Words like *air, sand,* and *oil* cannot be pluralized.

> *Example:* The *water* we drink has many chemicals.

Words such as these are called *concrete nouns* (nouns representing things we can see, touch, or smell). Even though we cannot count these nouns, we can count the quantities.

> *Example:* I drank three glasses of *water.*

A third type of uncountable nouns is called a *collective noun.* These nouns represent a group, for example, *audience, family, public, government.*

> *Example:* My *family* is very large.

When you pluralize any of these nouns, there is a change in the meaning of the word.

> *Examples:* a. *Love* is a wonderful thing.
> b. I have had many *loves* in my life.

Exercise 31.1

Directions: Underline the nouns in the sentences below. Next identify each noun as subject (S), object (O), proper (P) or common (C).

> ```
>                  S/P              O/C
> ```
> *Example:* Hawaii has tropical weather.

1. Mr. Jones has been a teacher for 23 years.

2. Next week the students will begin a research paper.

3. Beethoven wrote many symphonies.

4. My wife comes from Peru.

5. Each summer the family goes camping in Mendocino.

6. The air that we breathe is becoming more polluted.

7. The amount of money he lost in his investment was tremendous.

8. The grass was dying because of a lack of rain.

9. The last time Luke drove in San Francisco, he became lost.

10. Most of the technical components needed for the project must be shipped from Taiwan.

2. PRONOUNS

A *pronoun* refers back to a noun that has already been mentioned. Like nouns, pronouns are either singular or plural and occur in either the subject or object position in a sentence. Pronouns can also be possessive or start a relative clause.

Subject Pronouns:	I, we, you, he, she, it, one, they
Object Pronouns:	me, us, you, him, her, it, one, them
Possessive Pronouns:	my, mine, our, ours, your, yours, his, her, hers, its, their, theirs
Relative Pronouns:	who(m), which, that, whose, when, where

> *Example: I* went to the library to study when *I* realized that *I* had forgotten *my* book. As *I* was walking out of the building, *I* saw Mark, *who* was in *my* class. When *I* told *him* what *I* had done, *he* lent me *his* book for the day.

Exercise 31.2

Directions: Underline the pronouns in the sentences below. Identify them as subject (S), object (O), possessive (P), or relative (R).

>   P   S
> *Example:* <u>My</u> grandfather saw *Star Wars* for the first time. <u>I</u> haven't
>   R   O
> met a person <u>who</u> hasn't seen <u>it</u> yet.

1. He is a friend whom I visited last week.

2. Our instructor was worried that the class didn't understand her lecture.

3. They have one son and five daughters who spoil him rotten.

4. If Steve understood economics better, he could help you with your homework.

5. I have always turned in my homework on time.

6. When I saw her at the reunion, I didn't recognize her as my girlfriend from high school.

7. The person whom I saw you talking to yesterday was my college roommate.

8. My son was happy with the new puppy that we gave him last night.

9. She wouldn't tell me where she put it.

10. Elvis Presley, whose records made him a millionaire, was a legendary singer.

3. VERBS

Every sentence needs a verb. A *verb* shows either action or a state of being.

> *Examples:* a. Jack *drove* to the movies.
>   b. Frank *appears* happy.

In sentence (a) *drove* is an action verb. The verb *appears* in sentence (b) shows Frank's state of being.

3.1 Types of Verbs

3.1.1 *Action Verbs*

Action verbs tell what someone or something does. They show either physical or mental action.

> *Examples:* a. The children *swam* in the lake.
> b. The children *liked* the cool water.

In sentence (a), *swam* is physical. In sentence (b), *liked* is mental.

3.1.2 *Transitive Verbs*

Transitive verbs are followed by a direct object. The words answer the question *what?* or *whom?*

> *Example:* She *gave* a book to her friend.

In the example above, the direct object, *book*, identifies *what* she *gave* her friend.

3.1.3 *Intransitive Verbs*

Intransitive verbs are not followed by a direct object. The words do not answer the question *what?* or *whom?* The sentence could end after the verb.

> *Examples:* a. She *came* quickly.
> b. She *came*.

In example (b), *came* can either end the sentence or be followed by a word that answers the question *how?*

3.1.4 *Linking Verbs*

Linking verbs join the subject of the sentence to a word such as a noun, pronoun, or adjective that follows. The word that follows the linking verb either identifies or describes the subject

> *Examples:* a. Pat *is* angry.
> b. He *was* the best player on the team.

In example (a), *is* links the adjective *angry* to the subject *Pat*; it describes the subject. In example (b), *was* links the noun *player* to the subject *he*; it identifies the subject. Below is a list of common linking verbs.

Common Linking Verbs						
am	is	are	was	were	be	turn
smell	seem	grow	become	appear	sound	get
stay	look	taste	feel	remain	been	

3.1.5 *Auxiliary Verbs*

Auxiliary verbs are also known as "helping" verbs. They are used to form the tense, voice, or mood.

> *Example:* Larry *can* play the guitar better than anyone I know.

In the example above, *can* shows present tense, active voice, and the indicative mood. Below is a list of common auxiliary verbs.

Common Auxiliary Verbs						
am	may	might	will	does	were	be
been	is	are	can	would	did	have
has	had	do	was	could	shall	should

Exercise 31.3

Directions: Underline the verbs in the sentences below. Identify them as transitive (T), intransitive (IT), or linking (L).

T

Example: I will make the appointment for tomorrow.

1. The students have been quiet all morning.

2. John seems calm despite the pressure he is under.

3. Pattie has gained the respect of her peers.

4. My three-year-old son feels shy in front of strangers.

5. I am taking fifteen units this semester.

6. He is an expert guitarist.

7. The material appears strong and durable.

8. The food smells wonderful.

9. I will need a new computer soon.

10. Julie will leave for home as soon as she finishes her finals.

4. ADJECTIVES

Adjectives are words that describe nouns. In other words, they modify the noun by giving additional information. Adjectives answer the questions, *What kind of? Which?* and *How many?* Adjectives can occur before the noun that they modify or after a linking verb.

> *Examples:* a. The *anxious* students began their test.
> b. Tom enjoys *extreme* sports.
> c. The students were *anxious* to begin their test.

In example (a), *anxious* modifies students. In example (b), *extreme* modifies sports. In example (c), *anxious* again modifies students because it follows the linking verb *were*.

Exercise 31.4

Directions: In the following sentence, put *one* line under the adjective and *two* lines under the noun it modifies.

> *Example:* Our attic is filled with dusty antiques.

1. The school choir will perform a concert next week.

2. A cold wind blew in from Alaska.

3. My friend is excited about his trip to Iowa.

4. My favorite vegetable is Japanese eggplant.

5. I'll never forget the look of total surprise on her face when it was announced that she won a sizable scholarship.

6. The chocolate cake is delicious.

7. The devastating flood left over one thousand families homeless.

8. My older sister gave me a soft, fluffy kitten for my birthday.

9. Our new mayor is an eloquent speaker.

10. Sudden, intense anger is an emotion often responsible for starting a heart attack.

5. ADVERBS

Adverbs modify verbs, adjectives, other adverbs, or the entire sentence. Adverbs answer the questions *Where? When? How? How much? How often?* and *To what extent?* They can be a single word, a phrase, or a clause.

> Examples: a. Jackie did *very well* on the test *last week.*
> b. Frank is *extremely* good at playing chess.
> c. John plays tennis *in the park every Saturday.*
> d. *When I was in Hawaii,* I tried to surf.

In example (a) *very* modifies to what extent Jackie played *well, well* modifies how Jackie did and *last week* modifies when she took the test. In example (b), *extremely* modifies good. In example (c), *in the park* modifies where John plays tennis, and *every Saturday* modifies how often he plays. Finally, in example (d), *When I was in Hawaii* modifies when I tried to surf.

Exercise 31.5

Directions: Underline the adverbs in the sentences below.

> *Example:* He was <u>pleasantly</u> surprised.

1. David reluctantly agreed to lend me fifty dollars.

2. Yesterday we went to see *Planet of the Apes.*

3. During the winter break, we will go skiing in Tahoe.

4. It is extremely difficult to get my sister to hurry in the morning.

5. The instructor spoke quickly and enthusiastically about the next project we will be doing.

6. I recently began taking yoga classes on Wednesday evening.

7. I have never had the opportunity to go to Hawaii.

8. While I was shopping last week, I ran into my old friend, Jake.

9. When you see him, tell Frank to call me.

10. Usually, I drink a cup of tea before going to bed.

6. ARTICLES

An *article* is a word that comes before a noun and makes a word either specific (the) or nonspecific (a, an).

> *Examples:* a. *The* person I would like to meet the most is Thomas Jefferson.
> b. If you have murophobia, you are *a* person who is afraid of mice.

In example (a), the person refers to one specific person in the world. In (b) *a* person refers to any person in the world.

7. PREPOSITIONS

A *preposition* is a word or group of words that occurs before a noun or a pronoun and shows that word's relationship to the other words in the sentence. The noun is called the *object of the preposition.* Together, the preposition and the noun are called a *prepositional phrase.* There are three types of prepositions: *simple* (in, on, up, down), *compound* (within, throughout, outside), and *phrasal* (together with, by means of, in spite of). Prepositional phrases function as either an adverb or an adjective in the sentence.

> *Examples:* a. Paul will meet Sally *at* the mall.
> b. My dog stays *alongside of* me *without* a leash when we go on walks.
> c. Students *from* other countries are usually quite good at English grammar.

In example (a), *at* shows the relationship between the verb *meet* and the object of the preposition *mall.* In example (b), the two prepositional phrases are used as adverbs. *Alongside of me* is used as an adverb that shows where the dog stays, and *without a leash* shows how the dog stays. In example (c), *from other countries* is an adjective that modifies students.

Exercise 31.6

Directions: Underline the prepositional phrases in the sentences below.

> *Example:* Last Friday night, I went to the movies <u>with my friend</u>.

1. I usually drive my car to work.

2. What is the most popular sport in your community?

3. Larry finally moved to the head of the line.

4. Most of the students did well on the last test.

5. In college, your instructor may want you to think of your own topic for a research paper.

6. In the past few years, a number of states have begun allowing physician assistants and nurse-practitioners to write prescriptions.

7. She was shopping for a present for her father all afternoon.

8. I am looking for a new car with a lot of extras and safety features.

9. On the way to the airport, we passed by the new stadium.

10. In today's schools, there is an argument as to whether or not we should separate students with learning disabilities from students without learning disabilities.

8. CONJUNCTIONS

Conjunctions join words or ideas. There are two types of conjunctions: coordinating and subordinating. *Coordinating conjunctions* join two words or ideas of equal importance.

> *Examples:* a. Maria *and* Hector went snowboarding during the winter break.
> b. I want to go to the mall today, *but* I need to finish my homework first.

In example (a), *and* joins the two proper nouns *Maria* and *Hector.* In example (b), *but* joins two independent clauses of equal importance.

Subordinating conjunctions join an independent clause to a dependent clause. The conjunction is placed at the beginning of the dependent clause and shows that the dependent clause is less important.

> *Examples:* a. I wasn't able to buy the new Adrian Blau CD *because* it was sold out.
> b. *Since* I started college, I haven't had enough free time to relax.

The combining can be done in two ways as shown above. Be sure to punctuate correctly. (See Chapter 33.)
Below is a list of coordinating conjunctions and subordinating conjunctions.

Coordinating Conjunctions		Subordinating Conjunctions			
and	or	after	as soon as	in order to	until
but	so	although	because	since	when
for	yet	as though	before	though	whenever
nor		as long as	if	unless	while

Exercise 31.7

Directions: Combine the sentences below using either coordinating or subordinating conjunctions. (There is more than one correct way.)

1. We traveled around the world. We slept in many strange places.

2. He would rather ski than work. He has no choice.

3. You can't get in to the dance club. You are eighteen.

4. I don't like vegetables. I don't like dairy products.

5. I have been camping many times before. I have never seen a bear.

6. I was going to call you last night. My roommate was on the phone for three hours.

7. John went to the ATM after class. He took out some money. He would have enough money for the weekend.

8. I am a careful driver. I had an accident last week.

9. Moua will finish his B.A. this semester. He will immediately start work on his Master's degree.

10. The teacher gave us directions before the exam. Her directions were confusing.

CHAPTER 32

The Basics of Sentence Structure

1. Sentences
   1.1 Clauses
       1.1.1 Independent Clauses
       1.1.2 Dependent Clauses
   1.2 Phrases

2. Sentence Structure
   2.1 Fragments
       2.1.1 Identifying Key Words
             That Begin a Fragment
   2.2 Run-Ons

Good writers need to be able to analyze their work, not only for content but also for how the sentences are put together. To do this effectively, you will need to understand sentence structure and its terms. This will benefit you in class and peer discussions as well as when you work alone.

1. SENTENCES

A *sentence* is a group of related words with a subject and a verb that expresses a compete thought. The *subject* is the person, place, thing, or idea that performs the action of the sentence. The *verb* shows the action of the subject.

> Examples: a. *Turquoise are* semi-precious stones.
> b. *Jewelers use* turquoise in a variety of ways.

In examples (a) and (b), *turquoise* and *jewelers* are the subjects of the sentences. *Are* and *use* are the verbs.

1.1 Clauses

A *clause* is a group of related words that contain a subject and verb. Every sentence contains one or more clauses. There are two types of clauses: independent and dependent.

1.1.1 *Independent Clauses*

An *independent clause* expresses a complete thought. It can stand alone as a sentence.

> Examples: a. Labrador Retrievers are loyal dogs.
> b. Steven likes pizza.

Both of these independent clauses have a subject, *Labrador Retrievers* and *Steven,* and a verb, *are* and *likes.* Therefore, they are complete sentences.

1.1.2 *Dependent Clauses*

Dependent clauses also have a subject and a verb. However, they can not stand alone as a complete sentence because they do not express a complete thought. A dependent clause must be joined to an independent clause.

> Examples: a. when Mario was eight
> b. after you write this essay

Examples (a) and (b) do not express a complete idea. If they were left alone, a reader would ask "What happened to Mario when he was eight?" and "What do I do after I write this essay?" In order to express complete ideas, they must be joined to an independent clause.

> Examples: a. *When Mario was eight,* his family moved to Fresno.
> b. Make sure to look over your work *after you write this essay.*

Now that the dependent clauses have been joined to independent clauses, the ideas are complete. Dependent clauses can be placed at the beginning, middle, or end of a sentence.

> *Examples:* a. *After I paid my tuition,* I haven't had money to go out.
> b. The students *who received an 'A' on the test* can leave early.
> c. You need to read the contract *carefully before you make any decisions.*

Dependent clauses are also called *subordinate clauses,* which means that the information contained in the dependent clause is considered less important than the information in the independent clause.

1.2 Phrases

Phrases are a group of related words that *do not have* a subject and a verb. As with dependent clauses, they cannot stand alone as a sentence. They need to be joined to an independent or a dependent clause. Phrases are similar to dependent clauses in that they convey less important information and can be placed at the beginning, middle, or end of the sentence.

> *Examples:*
> a. in the living room.   I left my book *in the living room.*
> b. angry and resentful   The man, *angry and resentful,* denied any wrong doing.
> c. while paying the bills   *While paying the bills,* Bill gets quite upset.

Exercise 32.1

Underline each of the clauses in the sentences below. Next, identify each clause as an independent clause (IC), dependent clause (DC), or phrase (P).

>   DC   IC   P
> *Example:* <u>While I was driving to work,</u> <u>I nearly had an accident</u> <u>at the corner of Palm and Marks.</u>

1. We have still not been to the top of the Empire State Building, even though we have been in New York for a week.

2. When the doctor was paged, he left immediately.

3. If I were in charge, I would eliminate all dues from this club.

4. I have moved to three different apartments during the school year.

5. The police car turned the corner with a loud screech.

6. While traveling through Mexico, we visited both the Aztec and Mayan ruins.

7. The victim was in critical condition when he arrived at the hospital after the boating accident.

8. Lawrence always complains about doing his chores, but his sister never does.

9. Feeling confident and hopeful, the contestants were ready to start the game.

10. The phoenix, which is a mythical bird, rises from its own ashes after burning.

2. SENTENCE STRUCTURE

In conversation we usually do not speak in complete sentences. Instead we speak in fragments and run-ons. Naturally, no one mentions punctuation. Consider the example below.

Speaker A: "Hey, want to take in a movie?"
Speaker B: "Not now. Too much homework for tomorrow."

In a normal conversation, this short dialog would not seem wrong. Unfortunately, many students write in the same manner as they speak. However, your writing, although a reflection of speech, will not be well-understood unless you follow strict sentence structure and punctuation patterns. This section will discuss how to avoid three common problems writers have: fragments, run-ons, and comma splices.

2.1 Fragments

A *fragment* is a group of related words. It does not express a complete thought, yet it is punctuated as if it were. A fragment could be the result of writing a dependent clause, a phrase, or simply forgetting to include a subject or verb in the sentence.

Examples: a. In the next aisle. (phrase)
b. Shopping in a hurry before Christmas. (missing subject and/or verb)
c. I was about to pay the dinner tab. When I realized I left my wallet at home.
(independent clause)   (dependent clause)

There are two thoughts to keep in mind when editing your writing for fragments. First, make sure each sentence has a complete subject and verb. Example (a) is a prepositional phrase that does not have a subject or verb. Example (b) is missing a subject and a verb. Make sure you haven't punctuated a dependent clause as if it were a complete idea. Example (c) begins with the subordinating conjunction *when*, therefore creating a dependent clause. Usually, a dependent clause can be connected to an independent clause that comes before or follows it. Consider these corrections.

Examples: a. *You will find the spices* in the next aisle.
b. *I was* shopping in a hurry before Christmas.
c. *I was about to pay the dinner tab* when I realized I left my wallet at home.

2.1.1 *Identifying Key Words That Begin a Fragment*

Although there are many ways to begin a fragment, the following should signal a warning for a possible fragment.

Fragments Starting with Subordinating Conjunctions

If you start a sentence with a subordinating conjunction, you have formed a dependent clause. As mentioned before, to correct this fragment, you must connect it to an independent clause. (For a list of subordinating conjunctions, see Chapter 31.)

Examples:
Incorrect: When my brother comes to visit. We will spend time at the beach.
Correct: When my brother comes to visit, we will spend time at the beach.

Incorrect: I did not care which movie won the Academy Award. Because I never saw any of the movies.
Correct: I did not care which movie won the Academy Award because I never saw any of the movies.

Fragments Starting with Prepositions

If you begin a sentence with a preposition, make sure that there is a subject and a verb. Forgetting either the subject or verb will result in a fragment.

Examples:
Incorrect: With a little help. I was able to complete the project.
Correct: With a little help, I was able to complete the project.

Incorrect: I spent the afternoon working. In my garden.
Correct: I spent the afternoon working in my garden.

Fragments Starting with Verbals

Verbals are verbs being used as a noun. There are two types of verbals, *gerunds* and *infinitives*. A *gerund* is a verbal that ends with an *-ing* and functions as a noun. Because a gerund is based on a verb, it expresses action or a state of being. However, because a gerund functions as a noun, it occupies the same position in a sentence that a noun does, for example, the subject or object. If you begin a sentence with a gerund, make sure that you include a verb.

Examples:
Incorrect: Cooking dinner for my roommates.
Correct: Cooking dinner for my roommates is a thankless job.

Incorrect: Flying across the continent.
Correct: I enjoy flying across the continent.

An *infinitive* is a verbal consisting of the word *to* plus a verb, and it functions as a noun, adjective, or adverb. Like a gerund, an infinitive expresses action or a state of being, and if it is functioning as a noun, it occupies the same position in a sentence that a noun does, as the subject or object.

Examples:
Incorrect: To watch her children while she went to the store.
Correct: My sister asked me to watch her children while she went to the store.

Incorrect: To use correct grammar.
Correct: To use correct grammar is important.

Exercise 32.2

Below are ten fragments. Identify what type of fragment was made. Use (P) for phrase, (MS) for missing subject, (MV) for missing verb, and (DC) for dependent clause. Next, change the fragment into a complete sentence.

Example: P Under the bed. I found my textbook under the bed.

1. _____ When a person is not paying attention.

2. _____ After a short break.

3. _____ Planning my vacation.

4. _____ Due to the fact that today is the hottest day so far this summer.

5. _____ Because the campus is so large.

6. _____ To have enough money for tuition.

7. _____ Then walked out of the room.

8. _____ Being quite peaceful.

9. _____ Since I don't have a job.

10. _____ His project and handed it in early.

2.2   Run-Ons

A *run-on* is two or more independent clauses that are joined incorrectly. There are two types of run-on. The first type is a *fused sentence*. Such run-ons are made when no punctuation, such as a period, colon, semicolon, is used between the two independent clauses.

> *Example:* All small boats must return to port immediately they may sink in the hurricane that is approaching the bay.

In the example, there are two independent clauses that are not separated by correct punctuation. The first one is *All small boats must return to port immediately* and the second is *they may sink in the hurricane that is approaching the bay.*

The second and most common type of run-on is the *comma splice,* which occurs when a comma separates two independent clauses.

> *Example:* All small boats must return to port immediately, they may sink in the hurricane that is approaching the bay.

There are five ways to correct a run-on sentence.

1. Add a period between the two independent clauses.
   All small boats must return to port immediately. They may sink in the hurricane that is approaching the bay.
2. Place a comma and coordinating conjunction between the two independent clauses.
   All small boats must return to port immediately, *or* they may sink in the hurricane that is approaching the bay.
   (The coordinating conjunctions are: for, and, nor, but, or, yet, so)
3. Place a semicolon between the two clauses.
   All small boats must return to port immediately; they may sink in the hurricane that is approaching the bay.
4. Place a semicolon, conjunctive adverb, then a comma between the two clauses.
   All small boats must return to port immediately; indeed, they may sink in the hurricane that is approaching the bay.
5. Change one of the clauses into a dependent clause.
   Unless all small boats return to port immediately, they may sink in the hurricane that is approaching the bay.

Exercise 32.3

Each of the sentences below is a run-on. Correct each one using one or more of the five ways discussed.

1. Social science texts tend to be highly factual it is easy to get lost in detail and to lose sight of the general topics with which the discipline is concerned.

2. There are two types of people in the world, there are those that love horror movies and those that don't.

3. Antiques are very interesting to Jeff he watches the antique shows on TV.

4. Parasites are some of man's most ancient enemies they are once again emerging as a health threat in the United States.

5. The federal government has planned to extend protections for laboratory animals, such as mice, rats, and birds they are seeking to ensure that they get adequate space, air, food, water, clean cages, and feel as little pain as necessary.

6. Biology is the study of plants and animals it is all about nature.

7. Argentina is a country in South America, Buenos Aires is its capital and is considered one of the most exciting cities in the world.

8. Jake plays three different musical instruments: piano, violin, and guitar, he is considered a gifted musician.

9. Homelessness is a major social problem in the United States finding a solution has been difficult.

10. Sally and Bill went to the store and bought sandwiches, chips, and sodas afterwards they went to the lake and had a picnic.

Exercise 32.4

Select one of the essays you are currently writing for one of your classes. Carefully read it over to look for fragments and run-ons and correct them.

CHAPTER 33

The Basics of Punctuation

1. End Punctuation
   1.1 Declarative Sentences
   1.2 Interrogative Sentences
   1.3 Imperative Sentences
   1.4 Exclamatory Sentences
2. Commas
   2.1 The Eight Comma Rules
   2.2 Misuse of Commas
3. Colons
   3.1 Misuse of Colons

4. Semicolons
   4.1 Misuse of Semicolons
5. Other Punctuation
   5.1 Quotations
   5.2 Brackets
   5.3 Dashes
   5.4 Parenthesis
   5.5 Apostrophes

1. END PUNCTUATION

English has four sentence patterns which require different types of punctuation.

1.1 Declarative Sentences

A *declarative* sentence states basic information. It ends with a period.

> *Examples:* The world is round.
> Linguistics is the study of language.

1.2 Interrogative Sentences

An *interrogative* sentence asks a question and ends with a question mark.

> *Examples:* Have you been to Monterey lately?
> Can you recommend a good book to read?

1.3 Imperative Sentences

An *imperative* sentence gives a command. It ends with a period or an exclamation point.

> *Examples:* Do your homework.
> Go home!

1.4 Exclamatory Sentences

An *exclamatory* sentence expresses a strong emotion or feeling and ends with an exclamation point.

> *Examples:* Joanna yelled, "I need your help, now!"
> Watch out!

2. COMMAS

Commas are used to help avoid confusion in reading a sentence.

> Confusing: When the family was eating their daughter Jane was feeding her carrots to the dog under the table.
> Correct: When the family was eating, their daughter Jane was feeding her carrots to the dog under the table.

Without a comma, you may first think that the family was eating their daughter, Jane. By adding a comma after *eating,* the sentence becomes clear that they weren't.

2.1 The Eight Comma Rules

To avoid confusing readers, it is important to learn the eight comma rules.

1. *Use a comma in names, degrees, titles, numbers, dates, and addresses.*

   Examples: Henry Cabot Lodge, Jr., was born on July 5, 1902, in Nahant, Massachusetts.
   Jennifer Barber, M.D., borrowed $25,000 to open her practice at 5350 N. Roosevelt Ave.

2. *Use a comma between two independent clauses joined by a coordinating conjunction.*

   Examples: I need to fix my car, but I don't know a good mechanic to take it to.
   Larry has been feeling down, so I sent him a card to cheer him up.

3. *Use a comma to separate introductory elements from the independent clause.* The elements can be in the form of a word, phrase, or clause.

   Examples: *Moreover,* you will need to estimate the cost of the project. (word)
   During the meeting, I was unable to present my solution to the problem. (phrase)
   If you answered No to the last question, then you don't need to answer the next five. (clause)

4. *Use a comma to set off nonrestrictive modifiers.* A nonrestrictive modifier adds extra meaning or description to a word. If you remove the modifier from the sentence, the sentence can still be understood. On the other hand, a restrictive modifier limits the meaning of a word. If the modifier is removed from the sentence, then the meaning of the sentence changes. Consider the following example:

   Example: Only people *who speak Hmong* can apply for the job.

   The clause *who speak Hmong* describes the people who can apply for the job. If the clause is removed from the sentence, the meaning changes.

   Example: Only people can apply for the job.

   If the modifier is nonrestrictive, then commas are placed around it. Consider the next example:

   Example: Moua Lee and Vang Thao, who speak Hmong, can apply for the job.

   Nonrestrictive modifiers not only can be clauses, but also phrases or appositives.

   ### Adjective Phrases

   Prepositional and verbal phrases that are being used as adjectives may be nonrestrictive and are set off by commas.

   Example: The state of California, *in the midst of an energy crisis,* has asked its citizens to conserve as much electricity as possible.

   ### Appositives

   Appositives are similar to adjective clauses except that the relative pronoun is missing. Like adjective clauses, appositives can be restrictive or nonrestrictive. If the appositive is nonrestrictive, commas are used.

   Example: Lack of sleep, usually caused by existing time pressures, can increase stress.

5. ***Use a comma around a word, phrase, or clause that adds nonessential information*** to a sentence, for example, parenthetical expressions, interjections, direct address, the use of Yes and No, and interrogative tags.

Parenthetical Expressions

Parenthetical expressions are words or phrases that are inserted into a sentence to give extra information. Commas are placed around them.

Example: Most of the students, *according to Dr. Wong,* are not putting forth enough effort.

Interjections

Interjections are words or phrases that interrupt the sentence.

Example: The movie lasted for, *oh,* two hours.

Direct Address

Direct address is when you insert the name of the person to whom you are writing into the sentence.

Example: Jeannie, what color should we paint the bedroom?

Yes and No

Use a comma to separate the words *yes* and *no* from the sentence.

Example: Yes, I will donate to your charity.

Interrogative Tags

Use a comma to separate phrasing that asks a question at the end of a sentence.

Example: It's a beautiful summer day, *isn't it?*

6. ***Use a comma to separate consecutive adjectives.***

Example: Jesse walked down the *long, dark* corridor.

7. ***Use a comma to separate items in a series.*** This includes clauses, phrases, and words.

Example: The war was fought *in the town, in the streets,* and *man to man.*

8. ***Use a comma to set off quotations.***

Example: Carrie said, *"I don't have enough money to buy my books."*

2.2 Misuse of Commas

Avoid the following mistakes when using commas.

- To separate subject and verb

  Incorrect: The President, asked congress for support of his new program.
  Correct: The President asked congress for support of his new program.

- To separate a verb from the object

  Incorrect: Larry took, the book home.
  Correct: Larry took the book home.

- To set off restrictive clauses or phrases

  Incorrect: The students, who received an 'A' on the test, can leave class early.
  Correct: The students who received an 'A' on the test can leave class early

- To separate compound structures when the second structure is not an independent clause

  Incorrect: Rita appreciates contemporary literature, and classical music.
  Correct: Rita appreciates contemporary literature and classical music.

- After coordinating conjunctions

    Incorrect: Sam would like to date Sarah but, he is too shy to ask her out.
    Correct: Sam would like to date Sarah but he is too shy to ask her out.

- To separate an independent clause followed by a dependent clause that begins with a subordinate conjunction, such as *before, after, since, if, because,* and so on.

    Incorrect: Carla has been too busy to call home, since starting college.
    Correct: Carla has been too busy to call home since starting college.

- After *such as* or *like*

    Incorrect: Manivong can cook a variety of Thai dishes such as, Tom Yam Goong and Moo Pud Pak.
    Correct: Manivang can cook a variety of Thai dishes, such as Tom Yum Goong and Moo Pud Pak.

- Before parentheses

    Incorrect: Sylvia started her business with very little, (a chair, desk, and telephone), but now she runs a profitable business with twenty-five employees.
    Correct: Sylvia started her business with very little (a chair, desk, and telephone), but now she runs a profitable business with twenty-five employees.

- After a question mark or exclamation point inside a quote

    Incorrect: "When did you get into town?," John asked.
    Correct: "When did you get into town?" John asked.

Exercise 33.1

Directions: Carefully read the paragraphs below. Add commas wherever they are needed.

Magdalena Carmen Frieda Kahlo Calderon known as Frieda Kahlo was a Mexican painter who has become well-known throughout the world for her startling self-portraits. She was born on July 6 1907 in Coyoacan a southern suburb of Mexico City. However she often claimed to be born in 1910 the year that the Mexican Revolution broke out. Frieda's father was Guillermo Kahlo a Hungarian of German origin and a professional photographer. Frieda's mother was Matilde Calderon a native of Mexico.

Frieda's early life was plagued by a series of illnesses and accidents. About the age of six the lively young Frieda was stricken with polio and nearly died. As a result her right leg became permanently thinner and shorter. When she was eighteen she was nearly killed in a bus accident and sustained fractures to her pelvis ribs right leg and foot and backbone and was pierced by a piece of iron. Frieda never fully recovered from these two tragedies.

3.   COLONS

Use a colon in the following ways:

- To separate independent clauses when the second one explains or restates the first

    Example: The cause of the accident was clear: the driver wasn't paying close attention because he was speaking on his cell phone.

- After an independent clause to introduce a list, an appositive, or some quotations

  Example: During my trip through Asia, I visited many of the major cities: Tokyo, Hong Kong, Saigon, Bangkok, Manila, just to name a few.

- In a business letter

  Example: Dear Sir or Madam:

- Between hours and minutes

  Example: 8:23 AM

- To show proportions

  Example: The ratio of teacher to students in kindergarten through third grade is 1:20.

- To separate a title from a subtitle.

  Example: *I Got It: A Five Step Plan to Getting What You Want*

3.1 Misuse of Colons

Avoid making the following mistakes when using a colon:

- After a verb

  Incorrect: The herbs that I grow in my garden are: basil, oregano, rosemary, thyme, and sage.

  Correct: The herbs that I grow in my garden are basil, oregano, rosemary, thyme, and sage.

- After *such as* and *for example*

  Incorrect: The book list includes, for example: *The Giver, Romeo and Juliet,* and *Catcher in the Rye.*

  Correct: The book list includes, for example, *The Giver, Romeo and Juliet,* and *Catcher in the Rye.*

- Between a preposition and its object

  Incorrect: My family consists of: three children, two dogs, two cats, and a parakeet.

  Correct: My family consists of three children, two dogs, two cats, and a parakeet.

4. SEMICOLONS

There are three common ways to use a semicolon.

1. To separate two independent clauses that are closely related but are not connected by a coordinating conjunction

   Example: Frank loves sports; soccer is his favorite.

2. To separate two independent clauses that are connected by a conjunctive adverb or a transitional phrase

   Example: Frank loves sports; however, he is not very good at playing any of them.

3. To separate items in a series that contains internal punctuation

   Example: Three important jazz musicians of the twentieth century were Louis Armstrong, a trumpet player; Duke Ellington, a composer; and Sarah Vaughan, a singer.

4.1　Misuse of Semicolons

Many students overuse semicolons or use them interchangeably with colons. Do not use semicolons in the following situations:

- Between an introductory phrase or a dependent clause and the rest of the sentence

  Incorrect:　During cold winter nights; I like to curl up in front of the fire and read a good book.
  Correct:　During cold winter nights, I like to curl up in front of the fire and read a good book.

- Between an appositive and the word to which it refers

  Incorrect:　Jordan asked his older brother; Gerry, to help him work on his car.
  Correct:　Jordan asked his older brother, Gerry, to help him work on his car.

- Between two independent clause joined by a coordinating conjunction

  Incorrect:　Jeannie usually packs lightly when she travels; and she always carries travelers' checks.
  Correct:　Jeannie usually packs lightly when she travels, and she always carries travelers' checks.

- At the introduction of a list

  Incorrect:　Make sure you bring the following for tomorrow's test; a Blue Book, two pencils, and a calculator.
  Correct:　Make sure you bring the following for tomorrow's test: a Blue Book, two pencils, and a calculator.

5.　OTHER PUNCTUATION

5.1　Quotations

The most common use of quotation marks is when using someone's exact words in a sentence. Follow the guidelines below when quoting.

Beginning the quote:
- Place a comma after the introductory verb.
- Place the quotation mark.
- Capitalize the first word of the quote.

  Example:　John said, "You did a good job."

Ending the Quote:
- Place a period at the end of the quote.
- Place the closing quotation mark.

  Example:　John said, "You did a good job."

There can be more than one sentence inside a quote.

  Example:　Monica said, "I have never been to Iowa. I hear the people there are friendly."

5.2   Brackets

Use brackets around words or phrases that are added into a word-for-word quotation.

>   *Example:* "It is his [Bush's] belief that the economy will continue to strengthen during the
>   next quarter."

5.3   Dashes

Use dashes to set off material that requires emphasis.

>   *Examples:* a. The city set a new record for homicide this year—54.
>   b. The reaction from the city—from shock and anger to indifference—was
>   broadcast on the evening news.

When typing, use—with no spaces before or after them to form a dash. *Note:* Some word processing programs will automatically turn a double hyphen into a dash.

5.4   Parentheses

Use parentheses around asides.

>   *Example:* Bush arrived at the capital for a pep talk with his most powerful allies there,
>   Republicans who (barely) control the House.

5.5   Apostrophes

Apostrophes are used in two ways.

1. They are used to form contractions.

>   *Examples:*   I am   I'm
>   you are   you're
>   did not   didn't

2. They are used to form possessives of nouns and indefinite nouns.

>   *Examples:* a. The student's book was lost.
>   b. Everyone's attention was on center court.

Add only an apostrophe to plural nouns that end with s or add an 's.

>   *Example:* The neighbors' block party was a lot of fun.

Exercise 33.2

Directions: The following is an excerpt from Mark Twain's autobiographical *Life on the Mississippi* about learning to be a steamboat pilot. All of the punctuation has been taken out. Put the punctuation back. There will be more than one correct way to punctuate the passage.

The face of the water in time became a wonderful book a book that was a dead language to the uneducated passenger but which told its mind to me without reserve delivering its most cherished secrets as clearly as if it uttered them with a voice and it was not a book to be read once and thrown aside for it had a new story to tell every day throughout the long twelve hundred miles there was never a page that was void of interest never one that you could read unread without loss never one that you would want to skip thinking you could find higher enjoyment in some other thing there was never so wonderful a book written by man never one whose interest was so absorbing so unflagging so sparkling renewed with every reperusal the passenger who could not read it was charmed with a peculiar sort of faint dimple on its surface on the rare occasions when he did not overlook it altogether but to the pilot that was an *italicized* passage indeed it was more than that it was a legend of the largest capitals with a string of shouting exclamation points at the end of it for it meant that a wreck or a rock was buried there that could tear the life out of the strongest vessel that ever floated it is the faintest and simplest expression the water ever makes and the most hideous to a pilots eye in truth the passenger who could not read this book saw nothing but all the manner of pretty pictures in it painted by the sun and shaded by the clouds whereas to the trained eye these were not pictures at all but the grimmest and most dead earnest of reading matter

Source: Twain, Mark. *Life on the Mississippi.* Boston: Osgood, 1883.

Exercise 33.3

Directions: Take one of your essays that you are working on for one of your classes. Read it over carefully for punctuation mistakes and then correct them.

The Basic Structure of a Formal Argument for a Research Paper

Traditionally, the classic college research paper has been in the form of a formal argument. Students are asked to take a position on a controversial issue and argue in support of it or against it. Formal argument has a basic structure, and knowing that structure makes formatting research papers easier. (Refer to Figure 22.1, p. 77.)

1. Introduction

State the problem or issue being discussed. Give any background information necessary for your readers to understand the problem or issues, perhaps by tracing the issue's history or causes. For example, if you were arguing the abortion issue, it would be necessary to mention *Roe v. Wade*. If you were arguing the cloning issue, it would be necessary to explain what cloning is. This section should be completely without bias—just present the facts.

2. Possible Positions

Most controversial issues are complex. Although it may appear on the surface that people are simply either for or against something, most issues are not so clearly defined. Indeed, most people do not take the most extreme positions on issues but prefer a position somewhere in the middle. In such cases, the range of positions that people take on your issue should be mentioned, again, without bias, just the facts.

3. Thesis Statement

After setting out the issue and explaining what the controversy is about, and mentioning the range of positions people take on the issue, then make your thesis statement. Simply state the position you are taking in your argument. For example, "Abortion should be legal, but only to save the life of the mother."

4. Body

First, state reason or point number one of your argument and discuss it. Back up the reason or point using information or quotes from your research. This may take a paragraph or more.

Then, state reason or point number two of your argument and discuss it. Back up the reason or point using information or quotes from your research. Again, this may take a paragraph or more. Do the same for reason or point number three of your argument. Use as many paragraphs as necessary.

Continue following this pattern until you've discussed all your reasons or points of argument. Start with your strongest reason or point of argument and end with your second strongest reason or point of argument (or vice versa). Put the other reasons or points in-between. Place your weakest reason or point in the middle where it will be the least noticeable.

5. Deal with Opposing Views

If there are any reasons or points of argument held by the opposition that have not been dealt with in your discussion, you must acknowledge them and refute them by challenging their information or their logic. For example, if discussing the abortion issue, you would have to concede that the opposition has a strong point because abortion is legal. However, you could argue that just because something is legal doesn't mean it is moral.

6. Affirm Your Position

Finally, affirm the position you are taking in your argument. Remind the reader what your position is and perhaps mention your two or three strongest reasons or points. Do not argue them again, just restate them. Then tell the readers what you want, whether it is simply to agree with you or to do something (like write their Congressman or Congresswoman or vote for or against something). Whatever it is, just state it directly.

By following this basic structure, you will lay out a good, sound argument that will be clear and convincing.